THE BIG BOOK COIN COLLECTING FOR BEGINNERS

The Complete Up-To-Date Crash Course To Start Your Own Coin Collection, Learn To Identify, Value And Preserve And Even Build a Profitable Business From Your Fun Hobby

GERALD J. ROBINSON

Copyright© 2023 By Gerald J. Robinson Rights Reserved

This book is copyright protected. It is only for personal use. You cannot amend, distribute, sell, use, quote or paraphrase any part of the content within this book, without the consent of the author or publisher.

Under no circumstances will any blame or legal responsibility be held against the publisher, or author, for any damages, reparation, or monetary loss due to the information contained within this book, either directly or indirectly.

Disclaimer Notice:

Please note the information contained within this document is for educational and entertainment purposes only. All effort has been executed to present accurate, up to date, reliable, complete information. No warranties of any kind are declared or implied. Readers acknowledge that the author is not engaged in the rendering of legal, financial, medical or professional advice. The content within this book has been derived from various sources. Please consult a licensed professional before attempting any techniques outlined in this book.

By reading this document, the reader agrees that under no circumstances is the author responsible for any losses, direct or indirect, that are incurred as a result of the use of the information contained within this document, including, but not limited to, errors, omissions, or inaccuracies.

JUGOSLAVIJA
GRAN ALMIRANTE MIGUEL GRAU
MAGYAR NÉPKÖZTÁRSASÁG
SINGAPURA
SINGAPORE
INDIA

Table of Contents

Introduction 1

Chapter 1
What is Numismatics? 2
History of Numismatics 3
Parts of Coins 4
Organizations for Numismatics 4
Modern Trends of Numismatics 5
The Works of Numismatists 5
The Significance of Numismatics 6

Chapter 2
Brief History Of Coins And Coin Collection 7
Coin Collecting as a Hobby Through History 9
Famous Coin Collectors you Should Know 9

Chapter 3
Understanding The Basics of Coin Collectin 10
The Different Types of Coins 11
How to Evaluate the Quality of a Coin 12
How to Avoid Common Coin Collecting Scams and Pitfalls 13
The Most Valuable US Coins you Should Know as a Coin Collector 14
The Most Valuable US Coins that are Still in Circulation Today 15

Chapter 4
What is Coin Collection? 18
Who Collects Coins? 19
Why Coin Collection? 19
Are You a Collector or an Investor? 21
Understanding the Terminology of Coin Collecting as a Business 22

Chapter 5
How to Collect Coins 27
How to Get Started with Collecting Coins 28
Top Expert-Proven Tips for Collecting Coins 28
Coin-Collecting Tools and Accessories 29
Locations for Coin Collecting 32
Types of Fake Coins 32
Cast Counterfeit Coins 32
How to Identify Fake Coins 33

Chapter 6
How to Preserve, Store, and Protect your Collection 35
How to Handle your Coin Correctly 36
How to Store your Coin 37
Causes of Coin Damage 38
How to Take Care of Collectible Coins 38
How to Avoid Rare Coin Scam 40

Chapter 7
Selling your Coin 41
Tips for Selling Coins 42
Top Seven Places to Sell your Coins Easily 42
Top Mistakes to Avoid when Selling your Coins 45
Selling Your Coins: When Is the Best Time? 47
Five Questions to Ask to Know the Perfect Time to Sell 48
Factors that Determine the Perfect Time to Sell 48
Frequently Asked Questions About Selling your Coins 49

Chapter 8
Buying A Coin 51
Top Tips you Should Know Before Buying your Coins 52
The Best Places to Buy your Coins 54
Common Mistakes to Avoid when Buying a Coin 55
Questions to Answer Before Working with a Coin Dealer 56
Best Places to Find a Reputable Local Coin Dealer 57

Chapter 9
How to Make Money Collecting Coins 58
How to Make Money Collecting Coins 59
Money-Making Strategies Used by Top Coin Collectors 61

Chapter 10
Top Mistakes you Should Avoid As A Beginner in Coin Collection 63

Chapter 11
Myths and Facts About Coin Collection 66
Interesting Myths About Numismatics 67
Interesting Facts About Coins 69

Conclusion 70

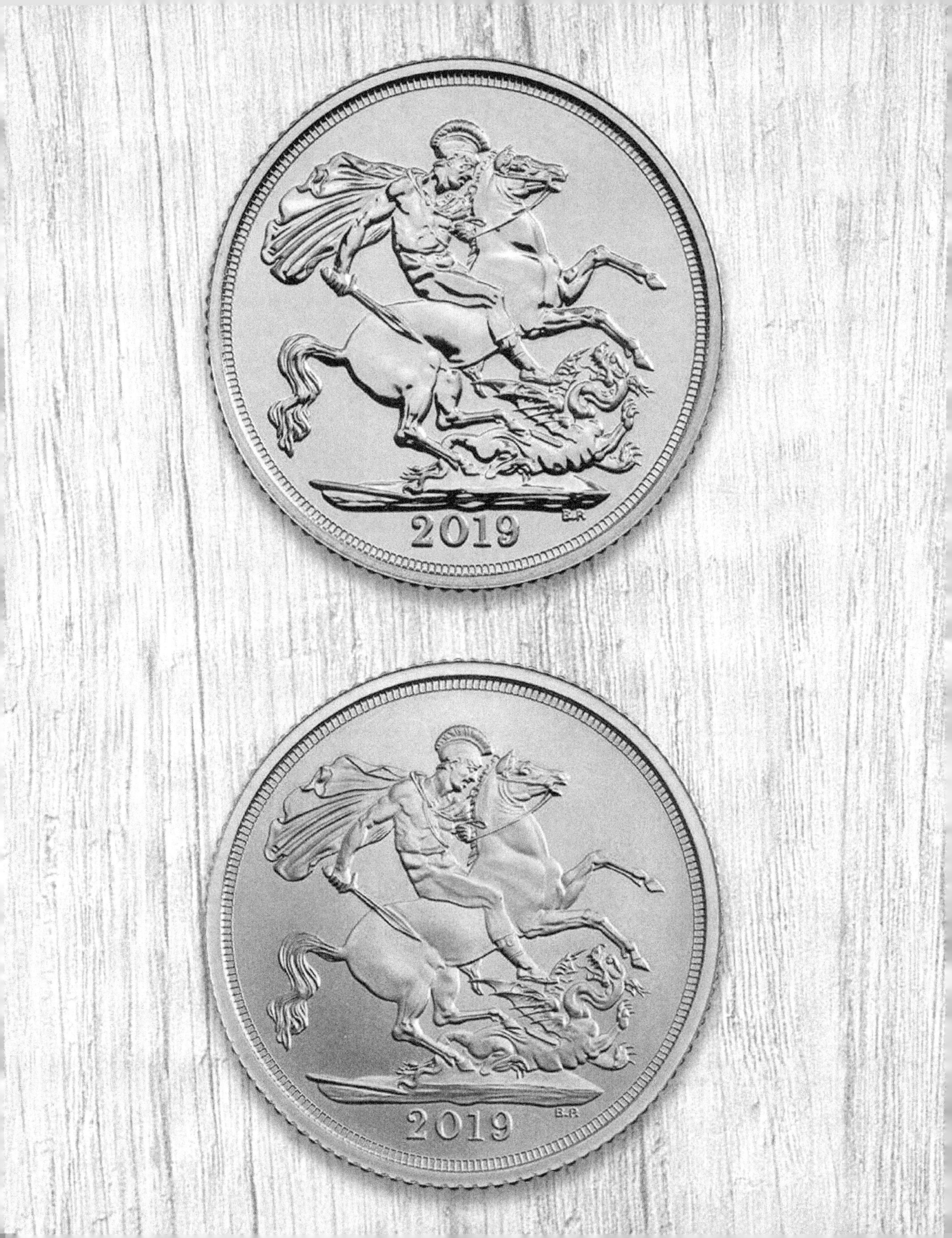
2019
B.P.
2019
B.P.

Introduction

Collecting coins or other legally made currency is referred to as Coin Collection. Coins with mint mistakes, rare coins, and especially historically significant coins are typical examples of coins collected by coin collectors.

Coin collecting is an enthralling hobby as every coin you collect is specially derived from a certain historical place, allowing you to create a connection with ancient times.

This hobby has been around for a long period and is adaptable at any age. It is relatively simple to start, as you can examine your current coins and determine how they integrate into your collection. Basically, coin collecting is an excellent way to spark an interest in subjects like history, math, and archaeology.

Coin collection and numismatics, the scientific study of currency, are two related but separate terms. Interestingly, you can start a coin collection immediately with the coins already in your reserve. They may not be worth anything at the moment, but they will possibly be sooner or later. Therefore, it's rare to go wrong with coin collecting.

The first Roman Emperor, Augustus Caesar, who lived over 2,000 years ago, was the first recognized coin collector.

Historically, coin collecting has different references; however, it became a trend during the Regeneration era and was done only by dignitaries. So typically, the average individual couldn't afford to do coin collecting, which earned it its name, "Pastime of Kings."

Currently, it has become a more accessible hobby and has resulted in some fascinating coin collections, including those of Pope Boniface VIII and Henry IV of France. Also, this was the time when regulatory bodies began to show.

Obviously, the best coins are ancient, the scarcest, and with few samples remaining. It can also be misprinted coins. Nevertheless, you don't have to own a collection of scarce or rare coins to enjoy coin collecting.

Notably, coin collecting is a pastime that entails collecting coins not only for their monetary value but keeping them for their arty worth. Hence, coins do not have to be old to be collectible; they could be foreign or merely artistically attractive.

Every coin has a story to tell; it's not just about where it originated. It cuts across these coins' best stories, which also represents their level of uniqueness. Factually, these stories are what best describe how such a coin is discovered.

Most coins can be graded, assigned attributes, authenticated, and encapsulated by commercial groups. Therefore, a coin's grade is vital in determining its value.

You can gather coins in many ways. One of the easiest ways is by saving coins you see in circulation—this is how most of the best coin collectors made their debut.

For example, some beginners quest for a coin of every date and mintmark variety to finish a group of Lincoln cents already in circulation. A coin's mintmark, a symbol or letter, categorizes the mint from which it was minted.

So, as new collectors learn some mintmarks and dates that are harder to track down than others, they might look for such coin dealers to buy from to fill a gap in their collection.

As I mentioned earlier, coin collecting has existed since the 12th century; but excitingly, it is still very popular to date.

Collecting certain £1 or £2 coins from extra change is one of the cheapest ways to start coin collecting. They will hardly lose worth, and you can decide to spend them if you're tired of the activity.

As you will learn in this guide, many inspirations can trigger starting a coin collection. For some holders, the zeal emanates from the ability to fully understand a superb work of art's weight, age, and history while having it in the palm of their hand. Others see coin collecting as a way of life instead of just a hobby or pastime.

Many collectors begin their coin collection journey based on their expected future worth. Some collect coins due to the metal variety, and others for the historical value of the coins.

Coin collectors may have a broad collection of coins from other countries, while others collect coins because they love checking dates and mint markings on their daily change and love collecting common coins.

Anyone can actually engage and benefit from coin collection, regardless of age. Many coin collectors started collecting cents or dimes as a kid, and many have made coin collecting a lifetime passion.

It first requires financial investment; therefore, joining an organization of coin collectors to gain ideas and help from experienced and skilled collectors is advisable. Also, you'll need someone to acquire your coins from and getting a reputable coin dealer can be difficult if you're new to the hobby.

So, having someone with long-time experience can be beneficial in guiding you to a competent and reliable coin dealer. Begin by acquiring a sizeable expanding lens and inspecting coins in a bright location to detect mistakes, mintmarks, and date reading on damaged or old coins.

Then, determine the coins you want to collect and buy a "bookshelf folder" for each. Also, you'll need storage, like clear coin tubes or plastic tubes with top screws, to keep your coins until you are ready to put them in a coin album; you can also use the storage to keep duplicate coins.

Based on dealer estimation or pricing, take note of the kinds of coins sold and how they're estimated. Also, you'll need someone to teach you how to evaluate a coin accurately based on its age, mintmark, surface, color, and state.

As you acquire more skill in coin collecting, your "eye for coins" will mature and improve to the extent that you'll be learning nuances and features like coin lettering, ensuring the letters are not blurred or blemished but remain visible. You'll be so captivated by the coin's common condition that you'll accidentally dismiss coins that show abrasion signs, missing out on the fun of coin collecting.

Coin collecting is a pastime that will exist throughout your lifetime. Your knowledge and skills will make and save you money when it's time, but most significantly, you will have fun while studying. Thus, spend as much time as possible viewing images, reading, learning from other collectors, and inquiring as much as possible from not just other collectors but also dealers.

Whatever your reason for collecting coins, it's not just a great pastime; you can potentially amass wealth or meet new people and exchange stories while collecting coins. It's an excellent way to make new friends!

So, it's either for investment purposes, as a hobby, or as a way of documenting history; coin collection is a relatively fun activity for various individuals. Discovery and having those coins will bring you so much joy, as every coin you add to your collection is an accomplishment. It's thrilling and enjoyable!

This ultimate guide to coin collection for beginners will outline everything you need to know as you go on this captivating journey of coin collecting. Also, it'll assist you in gaining insights into the kinds of coins to search for, how to get them, and other helpful information.

Overall, this comprehensive guide to coin collecting for beginners will teach you some basic principles that will help you build a collection that will suit your need and that you will be proud of. And without much ado, I can't wait to see you in the next chapter!

Chapter 1
What is Numismatics?

Numismatics is the study and systematic collection of coins. In a way, it is also called coin collection. The study of numismatics regarding coins determines how rare they are by researching their creation and use.

Although used for collecting different items used as money, such as tokens, paper, metal, checks, stock certificates, etc., representing current and past financial assets and liabilities, numismatics compares to coin collection.

Furthermore, numismatist refers to people who study the science of numismatics. These people are primarily interested in Roman or Ancient Greek coins, medieval coins, and modern minted coins.

Collectibles get their value from materials used, varieties, mintage figures, minting period, artistic designs, coinage errors, and socio-political context. These make them unique and valuable as an investment.

Over the years, numismatics, referred to as the "hobby of kings" judging by its esteemed founders, became one of the world's most popular and oldest hobbies. However, even though numismatics materials have become primarily commercial and economical, they also have crucial historical significance and artistic merits.

Coins are also crucial in archeology because they reflect the abnormality of a person when minted. Numismatics preserves and mirrors the social, economic, artistic, cultural, and political trends common at the time.

However, if a substantial demand requires their acquisition, the intrinsic numismatic value may increase beyond their current worth. Furthermore, since numismatics uses different materials, it offers a wide range of opportunities for recreation as a hobby and an inspiration for exploration and learning.

History of Numismatics

Numismatics was first used in English in the early 1800s. It was derived from a French word that means "of a coin." When linked to its Greek source from where it was borrowed, the meaning of the word becomes even more fascinating. However, the term later originated from the Greek name, "I divide or dispense."

The phrase was first used in the book De Asse et Partibus Eius by Guillaume Bude in 1514 and was the first numismatics volume ever written.

To understand numismatics, we first need to study the evolution of money. In human history, money has taken different shapes over time. In the past, people traded rare objects such as cowry shells, gold and silver, and other scarce materials.

However, due to these metals' heavy and valuable nature, the metal changed into paper money. In addition, there is evidence that makes the availability of specific coins of some eras questionable, which shows that many economic factors adversely affected the coins' production, including the demand and supply.

For instance, there was a significant reduction in coinage during the Great Depression, while production surged during the Second World War. Besides, many gold coins were melted when gold prices surpassed the coins' face value. However, these trends went out of practice with the economic revolution.

Unlike coin collectors, numismatists saw more value in coins. It was more than collecting these monetary tokens just for leisure. They valued these currencies, paper money, and out-of-trend coins differently and more deeply.

Numismatics first appeared in English in 1829, and many works of literature and academicians trace its origin to the early European Renaissance. However, the tradition of accepting money and other forms of payment dates back to ancient times.

The first Roman emperor, Caesar Augustus (27 BC to 14 AD), was one of the first coin collectors. Whenever Saturnalia, the festival honoring the deity Saturn, was fast approaching, Caesar would gather rare coins of different kinds and give them to his visitors as gifts.

During the early Italian Renaissance, coin trading became a vibrant industry. The most popular coin hoarder at that time was the Italian scholar and poet Francesco Petrarch.

European royalty and nobles, such as Kings Louis XIV, Henry IV, and Emperor Maximilian, started collecting old coins in the 15th and 16th centuries.

The academic field was supported by public collections and institutions in the 17th and 18th centuries. As a result, people in the area were more systematic and organized in their techniques.

In the 19th century, due to the influence of innovative technologies such as fluorescence spectroscopy, numismatists could study the tokens gathered and learn their histories. Numerous associations were also developed in the US, Europe, and Great Britain. Finally, the general people became involved in the trend because of occasions like numismatic conferences and coin exhibits.

Parts of Coins

There are some terms that one must first understand to analyze ancient coinage. Some of these terms include:

1. The Observe: This is the head or front side of the coin. Roman Imperial coins display the authority of the emperor or a significant relative. It can be challenging to identify the observation on Greek coins because of the images depicted on them.
2. The Reverse: It is usually the tail or back side of the coin. The Republican coins depict a theme glorifying a specific ancestor, while Roman Imperial displays some propaganda on the reverse. However, with Greek coins, it can be more challenging to identify.
3. Legend: This is the inscription on the coin, which is different from mint characters. It mostly runs around the coin's exterior edge, but exceptions exist. The legend can have abbreviations that are notable in the analysis of the coins. Some of them include the following:

- COS-Consul
- AVG-Augustus
- PM- Pontifex Maximus
- PP-Pater Patriae/Father of his country
- C or CAES-Caesar
- PERP or PP- Perpetuus/Continuous
- SC-Senatus Consulto/by a degree of the state
- SPQR-Senatus Populusque Romus/The Roman Senate and people
- IMP-Imperator/Commander
- PF-Pius Felix/dutiful to the gods, the state, or one's family

4. Field: This flat undecorated area sometimes contains mint or control marks. They are a sequence of letters or symbols showing who produced the coins.
5. Exergue: The space at the bottom of the reverse is often separated from the image by a line. Sometimes, this space houses a mintmark or part of the legend called the exergue.

Organizations for Numismatics

The study, exploration, and development of numismatic sciences are all pursued by several societies. For instance, The American Numismatic Society was established in New York City in 1858 to promote public appreciation of coins, money, and medals.

Since the association was founded, it has garnered more than 800,000 objects dating back to 650 BCE and has a numismatic library with about 100,000 books and artifacts.

Other numismatic associations include:

i. American Archaeological Institute.
ii. The Guild of Ancient Coin Collectors.
iii. The Society for Czech Numismatics.
iv. Association for Canadian Numismatics.
v. Israel's Numismatic Society.
vi. International Numismatic Commission.

vii. The Guild of Professional Numismatists.
viii. Society for Oriental Numismatics.
ix. The Australian Numismatic Association.
x. The Royal Society of Numismatics.
xi. The New Zealand Royal Numismatic Society.

Modern Trends of Numismatics

Numismatics has evolved from being just a hobby to becoming an academic field. Most people utilized the coins to study the history and culture of those civilizations, but the monarchs gathered them as gifts to give their visitors.

Modern numismatics entails the research of the production and usage of money and medals of the 17th century onward to regulate the relative rarity of the coin they study. The modern study of coins has become more accessible with the internet and modern communication techniques that make it easier to research the origin of coins and share the knowledge with other researchers.

Coin researchers and enthusiasts have established societies and local coin clubs to share history and ideas worldwide.

Commodities such as coins, tokens, paper money, and other means of payment still provide a window into a particular era's history, culture, and other economies.

Most importantly, they are worth acquiring because of their artistic value as engravings, although they have no worth as securities. Whether it is a coin, stock certificate, or note, analyzing them allows numismatists to learn much about the market's past and present state.

Numismatic coin collection is now considered one of the best foreign securities. The metal coins still have worth on the market. Therefore, it is wise to invest in old coins with melt value close to the worth of the mint metal. Commemorative coins representing certain popular events also command high prices on the market.

SUB-FIELDS OF MODERN NUMISMATICS

1. Exonumia: This studies tokens and other coin-like objects such as elongated coins, wooden nickels, and souvenirs. A large category of this study focuses on military awards and classifies these medals and awards by the military excursion or event they commemorate.
2. Notaphily: This is the study of paper money used as currency. Numismatists have gathered paper money since its inception as a form of physical currency by governments worldwide.
Established nations such as France, the United States, and Germany created notaphily in the 1970s.
3. Scripophily: This refers to the study and collection of securities like stocks, bonds, and certificates. Numismatists collect bonds and supplies because of their fascinating historical contexts and inherent beauty. These old bonds and stocks may include beautiful engravings they store as art pieces.

The Works of Numismatists

As I mentioned earlier, a numismatist is a person that specializes in numismatics. They deal with forms of currency every day as we buy and sell coins. They are primarily intrigued by the history of coins and currency and their production period. They include specialist dealers, collectors, and scholars who use coins and other currency as research objects.

Numismatists collect coins and currencies for research purposes. They study these objects from cultural, historical, and artistic viewpoints. They are different from coin collectors who only collect them as a hobby to complete their sets of coins.

The study of numismatics helped them to garner knowledge about the economy of that period and the civilizations that used them. However, coin collectors are very particular about collecting coins that indicate something important.

Numismatic coins are in various categories such as proof, bullion, ancient, rare, circulating, or commemorative. Due to this, numismatists have devised new ways to collect coins to add value to the economy.

The first group of numismatists mainly derived pleasure from owning monetary devices and studying these coins as exceptional amateur scholars. In the classical field, beginners' studies have achieved remarkable progress. For example, Walter Breen and King Farouk I of Egypt were renowned numismatists but not devoted collectors, and Harry Bass, by comparison, was a noted collector and a numismatist.

The second category is the coin dealer, often called professional numismatists. These people authenticate coins for commercial purposes. The buying and selling of coin collections by numismatists advances the study of money, and specialist numismatists are consulted by museum curators, historians, and archaeologists.

The third group is scholar numismatists working in universities, public collections, or as independent scholars acquiring knowledge about monetary devices, their economy, and historical context. Coins are relevant as a source in the pre-modern period.

The Significance of Numismatics

The study of numismatics is essential for reconstructing history, and coins offer reliable evidence for assessing history. Documents could have been tampered with, but coins may not be altered or modified. With numismatics, history can be evaluated more thoroughly, and supporting documentation can be obtained.

Many archaeologists anticipate coins while digging. The explanation is that it gives the strata they are extracting a date. Also, ancient Indian history can be found in coins.

Furthermore, information about the economy, trade, social structure, historical figures, morals, mythology, the military, and other significant topics can be found on coins.

Numismatics reveals historical events and practices. For example, each dynasty and monarch tried to create their own money. Their coinage style shows their personalities and also information on their beliefs and religion.

The comprehensive analysis of currency shows that India had many kings and dynasties. Coins also make understanding the artwork of that time more accessible. There are claims that antique coins are a work of art used in transactions when we view them. However, observing these currencies enables us to monitor the knowledge and technology they possess.

For instance, all the coins had punch marks between the 6th and 7th centuries BC and the 1st century AD. After that, molding was used to make coins. As a result, archaeologists sometimes come upon coins from several kingdoms. In addition, it helps to comprehend trading and communication across domains.

Earlier, coins were an equivalent of a newspaper. Romans used it to announce new emperors, win wars, celebrate holidays, and even sponsor charity causes.

Chapter 2
Brief History Of Coins And Coin Collection

Numismatics, widely known as coin collecting, came from the Greek word nomisma, which implies legal coin or currency. Now, we use paper notes, checks, and, more often, plastic cards, while the ancient world used coins for their daily purchases. The first coins minted were from Lydia in Asia Minor, which is now part of Turkey but was under the influence of Greece then.

The first coins were made of silver and gold alloy, dating back over 2,600 years. The then-Lydians were interested in business, and they were able to create a wealthy society that made developments in commerce and trade. Coins from this era show coin design progress during history.

Throughout those periods, the most well-known form of payment was pieces of silver and gold ingots. However, because no standards existed then and there were numerous unreliable merchants, every transaction involving gold and silver payment required a careful evaluation of the medium.

Coins were later designed circa 650 BC and minted using standardized gold and silver weights, and the government stamped them with a guarantee of value. In the next century, the development of coins became a primary means of business.

The coin-collecting hobby is believed to start as soon as the first coin was minted. Collecting them was a practical way to keep them because there was nothing like banks during those periods. Therefore, they were stored not just for their essential value but for their scarcity, and they have become a family legacy as they are passed from one generation to another.

Some scholars believe that actual coin collecting started in the late Middle Ages when several European kings sought out and amassed scarce coins used by ancient societies as tenders. One fascinating fact they discovered was that no two coins were equal owing to the systems of striking the coins. Coins were then struck by hand, and during the 1500s, coins started to be minted with machines.

Coin collecting gained fame during the Regeneration, and many enterprising individuals started creating high-quality forgeries. Presently, these forgeries are highly valued due to their age, quality, and historical importance.

The coin collection began when the first coins emanated and is considered one of the world's oldest pastimes.

In 1893, coin collectors, or numismatists, started collecting coins from mint facilities, and since then, the art or practice, as some call it, has increased as lots of coins have been minted. There are various mints in the United States, and on every surface of the coin, there is a small mark known as a mintmark, which represents the mint or city in which it was made. It may be trivial, but a mintmark is among the factors determining a coin's value.

In the United States, the first coins were made of copper and were struck at the Philadelphia Mint beginning as part of the Coinage Act in 1793. Production during those periods was done manually, and coins were struck one at a time. The government finally opened more US Mint divisions. A system for mintmarks was created on March 3, 1835, to differentiate coins minted in each one. In addition, rules were set for detecting coins stamped at each branch to ensure control of all coinage and coin production was regular for all.

Modern coin collection entails the study of the coins of the mid-17th to 21st century. It was during this era that coins started to be struck using machines. As a result, antique coins attracted interest from expert historians, archeologists, and scholars because of their archeological and historical worth. In addition, the modern coin collection provides for collectors' and amateur fans' needs.

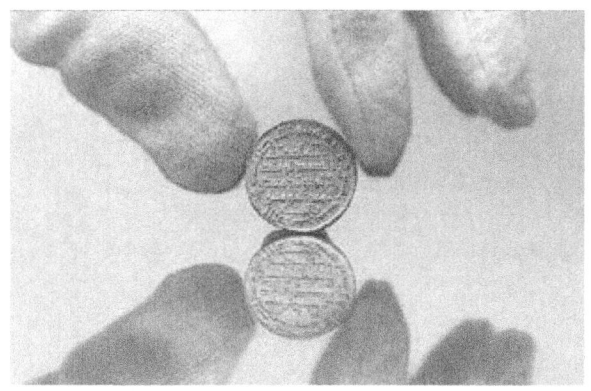

It emphasizes the determination of the coin's relative scarcity based on its making and use. Another crucial aspect of modern coin collection includes mint-made errors, coin varieties, mintmarks, the result of progressive die wear, and figures.

A set of collectors established the American Numismatic Society (ANS) in 1858 as a universal non-profit organization that maintains the study and security of coins and other numismatic supplies like medals and paper money. The most sought-after coins by coin collectors currently include the ones with historical interest, limited issues or errors, and memorial coins. Therefore, one of the most beneficial skills a coin collector can have is learning how to grade coins accurately.

Coin Collecting as a Hobby Through History

Coin collecting dates back to ancient eras and is one of the oldest hobbies on record. Roman Emperor Augustus loved to give inspiringly made coins to his friends. Coin collection has been a prevalent pastime for many great and famous nobilities in history.

These include King George III, John Quincy Adams, Thomas Jefferson, and Franklin Delano Roosevelt. They were all known to be actively engaged in coin collection. Another US president, from 1825 to 1829, John Quincy Adams, amassed and studied coins and used his idea to direct early American currency.

Coin collection was typically set aside for politicians and kings who used experts to scout Asia and Europe for coins of beauty and worth, which started around the 15th century.

The numismatic study was encouraged by dignities, and ancient sites' mass mines inspired the leading trade-in coins. King Louis XIV of France kept an extensive collection that he actively tended to daily.

The Victorian years saw the creation of many numismatic societies, and from there came an entire industry of dealerships and enthusiast magazines to support the hobby. By the 21st century, coins were an accepted form of investment, and gold and silver coins have become a stable point of investment in uncertain economies.

Today's hobbyists, just like Augustus, still treasure coins for historical merit and an immense sense of achievement.

Famous Coin Collectors you Should Know

Currently, coin collection is no longer regarded as a hobby for the upper class of today's society.

As mentioned above, President Roosevelt was a devoted amateur collector, just like Henry Morgenthau, Roosevelt's Secretary of the Treasury in the 1930s, coinciding with an era when stamp and coin collection was standard in the United States.

King Emmanuel III of Italy had over 100,000 collections of coins, which he gave to his broken country when he left the throne immediately after World War II.

Some of the world's most well-known and astonishing coin collections were put together by affluent private residents or families. However, a Baltimore businessman, Louis E. Eliasberg Sr., is possibly more famous for his comprehensive collection of circulating US coins gathered by mintmark. He remains the one person to have achieved such an accomplishment to date.

The 1849 US Double Eagle was the only coin that wasn't available in the collection, with the only known instance housed in the Smithsonian Museum in Washington, DC. The coins were sold after his death in the 1980s and 1990s and raised over $57 million.

The Farouk Dynasty governed Egypt for years and collected

over 8,500 gold and medals coins. Entertainers who regard coin collection as a pastime are Joan Crawford, Buddy Ebsen, Kate Hudson, Paul McCartney, and James Earl Jones, alongside sports superstars Andre Dawson and Wayne Gretzky.

Coin collection can be a gratifying hobby. Though it takes patience and time to accumulate the appropriate collection of coins, it can be a good investment for you and your generation.

The next chapter will walk you through the basics of coin collection, including the part of a coin, how to accurately evaluate the value of a coin, and how to avoid scams and pitfalls. It also covers the most valuable US coin you can add to your collection, which is still in circulation.

Chapter 3
Understanding The Basics of Coin Collectin

Coin collectors with interest in numismatics began somewhere. Coin collecting as a hobby may look a little bit confusing and scary to beginners. Some may even think that coin collecting is just for wealthy people with vast amounts of money. Nevertheless, many younger individuals from numerous demographics have lately shown interest in coin collecting.

This is because collecting coins isn't the only reason for coin collecting. One's drive for collecting coins may vary from another. You would choose the coins you desire to amass, combine, and then create your goal. Therefore, define your "theme" in coin collecting.

In short, as each collector might look for certain coin features for their collections, there is no wrong or right way to proceed with your search.

There are various coin collection approaches and several reasons one could start collecting coins. For example, many people started collecting coins when they inherited a collection from their predecessors. Other people began coin collection because they were captivated by the coin's history or saw a rare coin in their pocket.

The Different Types of Coins

Over the years, people worldwide have tested various items to symbolize value. For example, the early Chinese made copper money from knives. The citizens of Papua New Guinea valued the dried carcasses of paradise birds. Native Americans created and used wampum (clam shells, hand-crafted into beads, refined, drilled, and laced on leather strands) as an exchange medium.

All kinds of innovative techniques were applied to enable trading, but none was as convenient and essential as the small round pieces of metal known as coins.

There are different kinds of coins, and as a beginner, you might not know all the coins available to collect when you start numismatics.

Below are the most common varieties you'll see:

Gold and Silver Coins

Gold and silver are the basis for most great civilizations' currency systems. Egypt, Spain, Rome, England, Greece, the United States, and other nations all based their financial systems on gold and silver at one time or another.

Commemorative Coins

In the 1930s, many commemorative coin proposals appeared before the US Congress. While several of the currency bills had unreasonable requests, they became regulated. Nevertheless, the US Mint devotedly minted the coins, which traders sold with a premium above the coin's face value. The collecting community paid the premium for the coins and gladly included them in their collections.

Shortly, collectors criticized too many different coins and stated that investors were manipulating the prices and markets. Finally, the US Mint got the hint; the flood of tributes slowed to a dribble, and coin collectors were glad again. Nevertheless, many new people were interested in the coin collection of beautiful memorial coins, just like today's commemorative coins.

Overall, commemorative coins celebrate a significant occasion or pay homage to a distinguished individual.

BU. Rolls

In the late 1950s and early 1960s, collectors went crazy for BU. Rolls: original, bank-wrapped rolls of Brilliant Uncirculated coins. Collectors attempted to get rolls of as many different mintmarks, denominations, and dates as possible. As a result, specific issues, such as the 1950-D Nickel, were elevated to being uncommon, and prices shot up.

The public finally realized that coins with mintages in the millions weren't uncommon and wouldn't be—currently, the BU. 1950-D Nickel Roll is more economical than 35 years ago, and new collectors can't know why BU. Penny rolls from the 1950s are cheaper. The BU. Roll, just like every good trend, created many new collectors.

Silver Certificates

The old silver certificates' front says they are redeemable on demand for one silver dollar or silver later. But in 1964, it ended when the US government transformed the regulation and stopped silver certificate redemption.

Temporarily, the government permitted the public to redeem, in person, silver certificates for a certain amount of silver per note, either in bars or granules. But then, the silver dollar metal became more valuable than a dollar. Thus, coin dealers themselves were the lucky recipients of another windfall.

Immediately, everybody started searching their pockets for silver certificates to sell to coin dealers. As a result, several thousands of individuals who visited coin stores to sell their silver certificates became coin collectors.

Art Bars

Silver surfaced again in the early 1970s when 1-ounce silver art bars became very popular. Art bars are thin, rectangular silver bars with delicate surfaces and designs that commemorate just about anything possible – Thanksgiving, weddings, cats, a new year, etc.

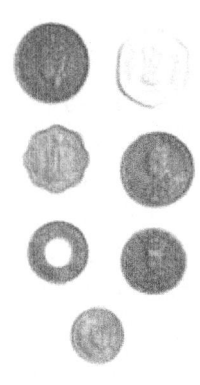

A flood of art bars stunned the market and quickly eliminated it. But, while it was in existence, the art bar craze caused many people to start coin collecting, many of whom continued.

Other Types of Coins Include:

i. Proof Coins: They are highly known for their distinctive, beautiful appeal, minted explicitly for collectors. Therefore, they are of the highest quality with a perfect design and finish.
ii. Error Coins: Any false coin set aside from other coins of the same design. These are often incredibly uncommon, hard to get, and pricey.
iii. Brilliant Uncirculated Coins: Because they have never been in circulation, they have an exceptional mint luster and appearance. A little lower in definition than a proof coin.
iv. Ancient Coins: These coins are usually handmade. They are incredible historical artifacts traced back to the Greek or Roman ages.
v. Universal coins: Any coin originating from a country other than the United Kingdom is called a universal coin.
vi. Bullion Coins: Coins constructed with precious metals like silver, gold, and platinum are called bullion coins.
vii. Circulating Coins: These are also called business strikes and are used daily.

How to Evaluate the Quality of a Coin

The process of evaluating the quality of a coin is known as "grading." Coins are graded depending on how young or well-preserved they are. While grades may be determined in different techniques, using the 70-point Sheldon Scale (or a modified variation) to evaluate coins' quality is quite common.

In previous grading systems, qualitative words such as Excellent, Good, Very Fine, Fine, etc., were often used. Unfortunately, it might not be easy to differentiate between terms such as Superb and Excellent, even for skilled or expert numismatists.

A more regular option is the Sheldon Scale, whose 70 points allow exact and granular evaluations of the special status of a coin. The last grade for a coin is (P-1) Poor, and (MS-70) Mint State Perfect is given to the one in a flawless state and hasn't experienced any handling at all. Between these two are various points, including:

- (EF-40) Extremely Fine: Though the coin displays some slight wear, the main features remain obvious, the writing is legible, and even the slightest information is discernable.
- (F-12) Fine: This grade signifies moderate but typically even wear, and the coin's writing should be highly readable.
- (G-4) Good: Though the coin is brutally worn completely, the essential elements are still clearly discernable.
- (FR-2) Fair: The coin is harmed brutally and has lost all the finer details, but the design's primary features are still discernable, and the coin can still be identified.

The above grades apply to coins that have been in circulation and have undergone some wear. The "About Uncirculated" (AU) group follows, which entails hardly used coins. Technically, they are no longer in a mint state, even though they have barely been circulated or used.

These levels contain:

1. (AU-50) About Uncirculated: The coin's design peak points show dim traces of damage.
2. (AU-58) Excellent Option Uncirculated: These coins can only have the minimum signs of damage or wear

to meet this grading requirement. Even though it has been handled, it is still nearly pristine.

3. Coins in a mint state that have not been circulated or handled once qualify only for grades 60 and more. Even out of the coins that have never been circulated, there are changes. Uncirculated coins but otherwise ordinary are seen at the lower end of the scale, while excellent coins are seen at the higher end. For example:

- Mint State Basal (MS-60): This coin does not have a lovely look even though it has never been handled; it may be lackluster and dull, have hairlines or contact marks, or have a bad strike.
- (MS-63) Mint Condition Acceptable: A coin with an average or less-than-average strike that has never been circulated. It might show blemishes or stains like a little dull shine or contact scrapes, but mostly, this coin is beautiful.
- (MS-65) Mint Condition Choice: This uncirculated coin will have good luster and an over-average strike.
- (MS-69) Mint Condition Almost Perfect: This coin is so nearly flawless that it usually needs a microscope to detect faults. Generally, a glossy, lovely, and attractive coin.

The coins on this scale are numbered from 1 to 70. It is worth noting that a coin with a lower number (like 40) may shine brighter than a coin with a higher number (like 60).

This is because the scale is divided into three major groups: circulated coins, closely uncirculated, and mint state coins. Hence, a high-quality circulating coin with slight to no wear and a general shining look tends to be extremely more attractive than an inferior, plain uncirculated coin.

You can evaluate any coins with this scale as a general rule, even if you're a beginner. I recommend getting a coin grading guide with examples to develop and improve your sight.

How to Avoid Common Coin Collecting Scams and Pitfalls

One of the most significant risks possible in coin collecting is falling victim to fraud. Unfortunately, some unreliable merchants are willing to produce information about the validity or worth of a coin, so you might not know the fact till it's too late.

Also, some dealers have more in-depth knowledge than others. So, you must know the fair worth to make informed judgments. For example, a new dealer may give original coins overpriced. Hence, education is the best preventive action to protect yourself from scams and other risks in coin collecting.

Research any coin you want to purchase before going to a merchant. Generally, looking for a dealer's review online is fast and straightforward.

The Professional Coin Grading Service (PCGS) and the Numismatic Guaranty Corporation (NGC) are independent grading services that you can use to estimate if a coin has been certified. These industries grade and examine coins before sealing them in tamper-resistant containers.

In my opinion, this other kind of confirmation is essential in ensuring that the coin you think you're getting is the one you are getting, particularly for new coin collectors. Then, the dealer's and market value can be compared by consulting the latest reference book to see if it is virtually comparable.

But note that an ancient coin's worth might widely vary depending on its market demand, uncommonness, state, and general historical status. So, it depends on you to choose whether a particular coin is "worth it" at a specific price if you're purchasing mainly for desire and fun rather than investment potential.

Alternatively, a gold bullion coin's worth can be better estimated. It follows the gold price, and sometimes coin merchants will value their coins, so you should check these grades carefully. You can see somebody listing their coin on eBay as Extremely Fine when it's just Good. To determine or evaluate if a merchant's stated grade is reliable, you must understand the grading scale.

You can validate that an authentic organization endorses dealers and determines whether a coin has been graded properly.

The Most Valuable US Coins you Should Know as a Coin Collector

As you progress in this art, you will see many coins in various denominations. Seven US coins are considered the most valuable in the numismatic world. Every coin collector that's interested in American coins should know these coins. Even if you are a beginner, no matter how you want to embark on coin collecting, I think you should know these coins.

Their identity is as follows:

The 1776 Silver Continental Dollar

When America got its freedom, almost immediately after the signing of the Declaration of Independence, the new United States needed something to honor and celebrate their freedom for the future. This coin had a brilliant design, ascribed to Benjamin Franklin. It involves a comical motif and the term fugio, which means "times flies" and "mind your business."

Additionally, 13 interlinking rings denote the various colonies. A large number was minted, but according to the centuries that have passed ever since, it is just normal that just a few can be seen. Finally, it is worth noting that the silver version of these coins is almost nonexistent; it is very rare to see.

The 1794 Flowing Hair Dollar

This is considered the first silver dollar coin ever minted by a US Mint. Its silver content is 90% and was struck in 1794 and 1795. Of all the coins today, it is believed to be the finest coin of its time. In 2013, this coin got a considerable sum of $10 million in an auction at Stack's Bowers Galleries. However, I can't say its precise worth as it regularly changes yearly.

The 1794 Flowing Hair Dollar is likewise essential, as it's the first coin dollar to be standardized all over the country.

The 1838 O Capped Bust Half Dollar

This coin is believed to have existed when the New Orleans Mint was opened—it was the first US currency to strike silver coins. This coin is precious to numismatics as it's very uncommon. It is generally believed that just 20 of these coins were struck. And currently, just nine out of these 20 survived and exist today.

Coin collectors do appreciate not just its scarcity but its design as well. Out of all US coins, the eagle representation on this coin is considered one of the most well-represented, not to mention its 13.36-gram weight!

The 1867 Confederate States Half Dollar

The confederate states took over the New Orleans Mint in 1861. They did not have precious metals in reserve to use in striking coins; thus, they decided to use paper money rather than coinage to support their hard war work. Nevertheless, there were limited confederate cents and half dollars that were minted. Unfortunately, no one knew about them until they surfaced in private collectors' hands after the Civil War.

1870 S Seated Liberty Dollar

No official record for this coin makes it very fascinating. Eleven traced samples allegedly exist, but there hasn't been an authorized validation that they are there. Of these dollars, the ones with an S min mark and a logo that they were struck in San Francisco are the most valued ones. All of them have a proportion of silver equivalent to 90%. If you see one of these coins, you will likely notice their wear state, as it's nearly impossible to see them in good condition.

The 1913 Liberty Head Nickel

Just a very minimal quantity of these nickels was made by the United States Mint, meaning that it's an uncommon coin that is specifically beneficial to modern-day coin collectors. It's described that only five Liberty Head Nickels are recognized to be in existence currently. Three of these coins are owned privately, while two are housed in museums.

The 1927 D St. Gauden's Double Eagle

Former President Franklin D. Roosevelt of the United States recalled all the gold coins. They were converted to gold bars or melted completely in circulation or bank vaults. This happened in 1933. Among those gold coins was our 1917 D St. Gauden's Double Eagle. They were one of the lowest mintage coins of the Gauden's Double series, with the original minted number standing at 180,000.

A few people did not return these coins during the recall, as about 11-15 pieces exist today. They were treasured then as gold coins, but the rarity factor has made them even more valuable.

The Close "AM" Penny

Why would a space between A and M in America make a coin memorable and worthwhile? This is because coins are minted very perfectly, and there should not be any errors. Therefore, any minor deviation from the exactness clasps the collector's attention.

A deviation occurred in 1992 when coinages were struck (in Philadelphia). As a result, the spacing between the "A" and "M" in "United States of America" on the penny's reverse was closer than regular. Therefore, the term "Close AM" was derived.

There are just five pieces of 1992 P- known to exist. Also, others struck in Denver 1992- D. Fifteen bits have been located. In 2012, one was sold out of them for $20,700.

The Most Valuable US Coins that are Still in Circulation Today

The kinds of coins listed above are rare because they are not available for circulation anymore. Therefore, you won't find them in your change in your store. Instead, most of them sit in prestigious coin albums of coin collectors, while others are resting in museums for people to appreciate. However, you can stumble upon one in an old site with your metal detector.

Now, if you've never come across those listed above, it doesn't imply that you won't have a worthwhile coin in your collection. Coins that are worthwhile or valuable are still in circulation to date. Compared to their face value, many commonly used coins are evaluated at a much higher price.

You may not have to buy them. However, you may come across them in your coin jar as they are very much in circulation.

Some valuable US coins that you can look out for include the following:

The 1943 Lincoln Head Copper Penny

This copper coin was struck during wartime when copper was seriously required for the war effort and wasn't used for coin making. As a result, the copper penny collection was made unintentionally. During this period, the most common coinages were created out of silver and coated with silver in a glossy way. During this time, very few of the copper coins left the mint, hence the reason the Lincoln Head Copper Penny of 1943 is scarce and could amount to up to $10,000.

The 1955 Double Die Penny

This is an exceptional coin with a double image due to misalignment during the imprinting process. In 1955, 20,000 of these coins were distributed in circulation, most released

The Big Book Of Coin Collecting For Beginners | 15

as change. This coin has a face value of $0.01. Therefore, if you stumble upon one in a good state, it could sell for about $1,800.

The 1969 S Lincoln Cent with Double Die Obverse

This is an excellent coin as it was the only one featured on America's "most wanted" of the Federal Bureau of Investigation list. However, note that fake ones may still be in circulation because fakers Roy Gray and Morton Goodman made very similar coins, attracting devastating attention from the authorities.

It is recorded that not more than a hundred original pieces were produced. However, due to its scarcity, it commands high value. It has about $126,000 estimated value in auctions.

The 1997 Double Ear Lincoln Penny

Abraham Lincoln may not have had flawless or relatively general features. He was exceptionally tall with a facial irregularity, to mention a few oddities. But he didn't have double ear lobes, even though his portrait in a mistake coinage indicated so. It was struck in 1997 and is usually referred to as the Double Ear Lincoln Penny. Numismatics are attracted to this coin because of the double ear feature, which makes it valuable and worth up to $250.

The 1982 No Mintmark Roosevelt Dime

The Philadelphia Mint mistakenly omitted "p" on the Roosevelt Dime in 1982, which implies that the mintmark is missing on this coin. The number released was not clearly stated, but about 10,000 have been said to exist. Its face's value is $0.10, but in the collector's world, it has an estimated value of $300.

The 1999 P Broad Struck Quarter

This quarter has turned out to be more valuable than its face value because of an error committed during the minting process; it has an estimated value of $25, while its face value is $0.25. The mistake was that the coin was "wide-minted."

"Wide-minted" means it was not lined up properly in the machine when it was minted. Hence, it seems to have an overgrowth on one part of the edge giving it an unusual look. Although some mistakes are hard to detect sometimes, it cannot be easy to notice them.

The 2004 Wisconsin State Quarter with Extra Leaf

If you are passionate about state quarters, this coin may be a very fascinating one to collect. In 2004, 453 million of this quarter were struck. Unfortunately, thousands, in some way, had, on the tail side, an extra leaf on a shell of corn. It is reported that a mint worker deliberately committed this error. Hence, the mistake makes the coin valuable to coin collectors. Furthermore, the extra leaf increased the coin's quality, amounting to $1499.

About 5000 of the quarters have been discovered in Tucson.

The 2005 P "In God We Rust" State Quarter

This is another error coin. The inscription was supposed to be "In God We Trust," but the letter "T" was omitted; instead, the term "Rust" was inscribed on the coin instead of "Trust." The mistake was not aimed at making any report about religion or government—the error reportedly resulted from grease buildup in the coin die when filling T.

This faulty coin is not that rare, so it may not be worth much in the market. It has a face value of $0.25, yet some collectors find it quite attractive, as the error is exciting, and it can be sold for up to $100.

The 2005 Speared Bison Jefferson Nickel

This nickel has on its back a buffalo that appears to be stabbed from beneath. The mistake happened when the die was cut during the coin minting process. Although it makes an elegant detail on the coin, it's not considered highly worthwhile. It has a face value of $0.05, but there was an exemption. It's recorded that a 2005 D 5C Speared Bison Jefferson Nickel was sold for about $1,265 at an auction.

The 2007 "Godless" Presidential Dollar Coin

All United States money has had the "In God We Trust" infamous inscription, but as of 2007, not all of them got to have it. Recently, the new George Washington one-dollar coins were distributed in the US.

An unknown number was said to be accidentally made without the infamous "logo" inscription. Generally, they are named "Godless" but are officially termed as "Missing Edge Lettering" dollars. Many of these coins have been seen, and their price is between $29 and $228.

The Roosevelt Silver Dimes and Washington Silver Quarters

Copper and nickel alloys were used in making modern-day dimes and quarters with no trace of silver. Nevertheless, before 1965, not less than 95% of their mixture was silver. These coins are common yet worth more than their face value due to their silver metal composition.

In summary, coin collecting is a fantastic pastime that anyone can do. You don't need a specific skill set or intelligence to engage in it. All you need is to be passionate about it. Nevertheless, it's worth noting that many individuals have started collecting coins for various purposes. But no matter your motivation, coin collecting can simultaneously be an informative and enthralling pastime.

It's pretty simple for beginners. However, if you get involved in communities or clubs, this might boost your knowledge. After all, it's usually better when you move with people who are as interested or even more passionate than you are.

Prioritized lifelong learning can also be of help in your coin-collecting journey. First, you must be current on trends and news in the coin-collecting world. Additionally, you must be ready to research and get informed with updates on the many forums you join.

I believe this chapter has enlightened you on all you need to know about the fundamentals of coin collecting. So, let's dive even deeper into what exactly coin collecting is in the next chapter.

See you on the next page!

Chapter 4
What is Coin Collection?

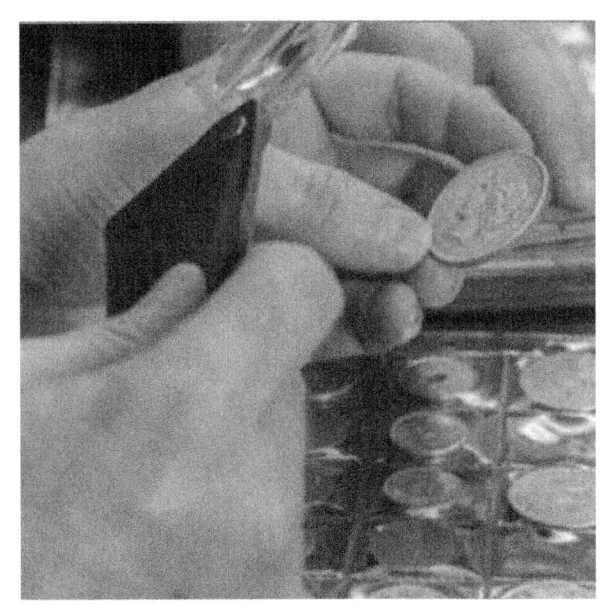

Coin collecting systematically studies coins, paper money, tokens, and materials of similar form and use. The art of coin collecting is one of the oldest pastimes in the world. However, except for Japan and China, the introduction of paper money has been a relatively new development since the 18th century.

Thus, while paper money and other note forms are collectible or valuable, the history of that form of collecting is unique from coins and is fundamentally a modern phenomenon.

Who Collects Coins?

Coin collection tends to be associated with the extremely wealthy. However, that's not usually the case.

Coin collection is now a hobby that can engage many people from several social strata, age groups, and overall interests. Anyone can be a coin collector nowadays, from kids to predecessors, artists, engineers, women, and men.

A COIN COLLECTOR COULD BE ANY OF THE FOLLOWING:

- A typical collector is ordered and stable and will usually not rest until they tick all the boxes on their list.
- An esthetic collector will primarily collect coins for their beautiful look. For this type of collector, the appearance of coins is sometimes more essential than their estimated worth.
- A speculator only collects coins to increase his investment. However, I don't recommend that you do this, particularly not as a novice.
- A perfectionist always looks for coins that are flawless at all points. This is because they want the coin to look perfect, worthwhile, and in a good state.
- The historian collector collects coins because they have bits of history. Since coins are living proof of the past era, this collector will develop a virtually emotional bond with them.
- The economical collector collects as much as possible and often looks for a cheap coin. The primary principle or determinant is price.
- The academic collector is sometimes a numismatist—at least to an unprofessional level. They don't just collect coins, but also their details. They do this in abundance to write a book on the topic.
- Another set of people that collect coins is the presenter. This type of collector does this to brag. He will construct a whole altar in his house for his coins and show them off at every opportunity to visitors.
- The patriot will primarily collect coins that bond with his country's history. But, most often, there's a possibility that the same individual will collect other collectibles related to his country.

Undoubtedly, you might develop into the kind of collector that doesn't fall into any of the categories mentioned above as time goes on. The main reason for discussing them was not to assist you in selecting a niche but to assist you in understanding that there are several kinds of coin collectors.

Why Coin Collection?

Unlike many hobbies that require a lot of money and effort, you don't have to go bankrupt to collect coins. Collecting coins costs nothing. Of course, you will likely put in some money to add a specific piece of coin to your collection as you progress in your journey as a coin collector.

But for that period, you must have learned the actual value of coins and how to purchase them to secure your investment.

The purpose of collecting coins all depends on what fascinates you. Here are some reasons people engage in coin collections:

TO EXPAND YOUR HISTORICAL KNOWLEDGE

Coins have archeological and historical value. Holding a small piece of history in your hands is extraordinary, whether it's an old coin with the portrait of Alexander the Great or a 1943 US cent made of zinc-coated steel instead of regular copper.

Historical coins have exciting stories to share and having such a coin ultimately makes you create or share a bond with the past.

The same can be said about pirate treasure coins and coins recovered from historic shipwrecks. In addition, world coins can help you learn about different nations and cultures worldwide.

AS AN EXPENDITURE

A coin's value is determined by a few factors and sometimes surpasses its face value. Some coins are expensive metals, and among numismatic professionals, rare coins usually command high prices—one can even realize millions of dollars from the most valuable ones.

INVESTMENT

A high-quality and highly sought-after coin can be a wise investment. However, if your goal is ultimately to sell your coins for an income, you must thoroughly research coins and market trends to select the best viable purchase strategy.

TO ENJOY

Many people enjoy and find pleasure in coin collecting. You may enjoy the rush of looking for an uncommon currency or completing a particular set or valuing a coin's beautiful and arty worth.

SERIES

Those who gather coins series aim to have one of each mintmark and date produced, which usually contains any main design differences.

The US Standing Liberty Quarter was made at the Philadelphia, San Francisco, and Denver Mints from 1916 to 1930. A complete set comprises both designs for those years and from each mint.

WORLD COINS

The most popular coin collection types are World Coins. People wishing to build a typeset typically want one of each series and the main design variation within each series.

PROFIT

Coin collections can be used for your investment portfolio diversification. An expert coin dealer can assist you in adding value to your portfolio by selling uncommon silver and gold coins. In addition, many professionals will say that investing in valuable metal bullion coins may assist you in cutting down your risk. Also, you can sell your coin collection if you need money.

FOR FULFILMENT

Seeing how things turn out is in our nature. When we see a job or a goal completed, it offers us a feeling of achievement. Successful coin collectors begin by determining what they want to collect.

After finding the perfect coin for their collections, the "joy of the hunt" sometimes excites us. Discovering a precious coin in your wallet can also give you satisfaction. Lastly, one of the most enthralling parts of coin collecting is the fulfillment of possessing a valuable coin collection.

LEAVING A LEGACY

A properly planned and well-invested coin collection can be a good inheritance for your children. While few individuals get rich by collecting coins overnight, well-thought-out and well-planned investing in precious and uncommon coins can rise in value over time.

Try to boost your children's or grandchildren's interest in coin collecting. Most children lose interest in coin collecting in their teens, though they may go back after several years. They'll probably be able to replicate your coin collection legacy later. They may even remember receiving a distinct coin from you.

RELAXATION

Having a coin collection and studying the history of a particular coin might assist you in eliminating the pressure and fatigue you experience during the day. Coin collecting is easy, as it can be found in your wallet or pocket, at a coin exhibition, at a desired coin store, or in cyberspace.

Also, coin groups all over the country can assist your coin-collecting pastime in becoming more enjoyable.

BEAUTY AND ART

Every coin design starts in the hands of a skillful artist. Though different kinds of artists can make coins, those skilled in relief sculptures are the best.

Most coin collectors believe that the most attractive US coin ever made was Saint-Gaudens Double Eagle, which was struck between 1907 and 1933. Other works of art includes Victor David Brenner's Lincoln Cent, Bella Lyon Pratt's Indian Head Quarter Eagle and Half Eagle sculpted in sunken relief, and William Wyon's The Una and the Lion on a British £5 gold coin.

As such, coin collections are art collections. The holder of a carefully curated coin collection will want to show off their valuable possessions proudly.

INVESTMENT

We love to gather stuff as kids, mainly coins. Everything is dear to us. Although most of the coins we found on the ground as a kid were invaluable, a few may be—and even considered investments.

Nevertheless, just like any other investment, you must know what you are investing in and understand that there is a possibility that things may not work as proposed.

Are You a Collector or an Investor?

If you are serious about becoming a numismatist, this is a crucial question to answer. An authentic coin collector collects coins for their inherent and acquired worth (numismatic value), beauty, uniqueness, and pleasure of the pastime.

They cherish the designs and images printed on the coins and get much satisfaction knowing they have collected a set. Moreover, they are concerned about the coin's history, how, who, and when they were created. But while they do like to collect coins for these motives, most collectors also have income as part of their goal.

However, if your overwhelming motive for collecting coins is to make an income, and you stack up gold and silver with the expectation that the coins will rise in value, bringing you a considerable income, then you are an investor.

If you have such an aim, it will be best for you to acquire bullion rather than collective coins, as you won't have to pay high commissions for their purchase.

Understanding the Terminology of Coin Collecting as a Business

Coin collecting is a time-honored hunt that people have adored for countless years. Numerous people confirm that there is something unique about searching for a valuable or rare coin and finally discovering it after searching for some years.

There's fulfillment in learning all there is to know about particular kinds of coins, plus it's fun to attend coin exhibitions and browse auctions online for those coins you're planning to include in your collection.

Nevertheless, coin collecting isn't always the most superficial hobby to hop into. For novices, the number of coin-collecting jargon and terminologies thrown around can be devastating, especially when coin collectors speak their language.

The beginner coin collector might not know the meaning of coin grading, what in the world a die is, or what a business strike means. This is where understanding the terminology of coin collecting comes in.

If you want to start collecting coins, you should be able to do so without feeling the inconceivable jargon barrier. So, to introduce you to some of the most common coin-collecting jargon, here are some basic coin-collector terminology you're likely going to run into as you proceed in your coin-collecting journey:

- Alloy: The mixture of two or more metals, typically to make something more potent and more corrosion resistant.
- American Numismatic Association (ANA): This nonprofit educational organization supports the study of money all over the world.
- Annealing: Heating blanks or planchets in a heater that unstiffens the metal.
- Assay: The evaluation of metal to determine its quality and content. A coin appraisal checks that coins have been made to the proper purity based on their specifications. This is especially applicable to silver and gold coins.
- Authentication: Reliable coin dealers provide an authentication service, certifying notable coins as accurately based on professional analysis.
- Bag Mark: Also known as "contact marks," a surface mark or nick on a coin, typically from contact with other coins in a mint bag. More often seen on big silver or gold coins.
- Beading: An elevated, dotted edge along a coin rim.

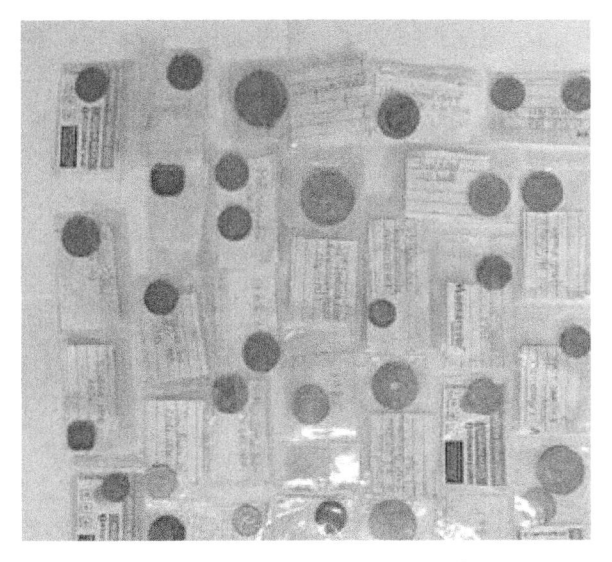

- Bi-Metallic: A coin that contains two different metals merged.
- Blank: A blank is a small disc of metal that has passed through a coin press with two dies. Dies mint the blanks with a strong force to turn them into coins, complete with a design on any side. The blank is a metal piece on which a coin design is printed.
- Bullion: Gold, silver, or platinum in the form of bars or other storage forms, including ingots and coins.
- Bullion Coin: Valuable metal coin traded at the current bullion values.
- Business Strike: A coin made for universal circulation (contrary to proof or uncirculated coinage explicitly made for collectors).
- Bust: A picture with the head, neck, and upper shoulders on a coin.
- Brass: A copper and zinc alloy, usually yellow and sometimes mistaken for gold. The antique Romans used brass for some of its metal coin bases, and it was often used for counters and jetons in the late 18th century.
- Brilliant Uncirculated: This refers to an exceptional standard. Commonly abbreviated to BU, these coins are struck to a higher standard than circulating and bullion coins. As a result, they offer a good level of design detail but with a lower definition than proof coins.
- Cameo: A vital distinction in the surface appearance of foreground devices relative to the field. Proof coins often exhibit this feature.
- Cast Coins: Coins are made by pouring iron into a mold. This technique was applied for the first Chinese "cash" coins, and ancient Roman bronze coins are hardly used nowadays because current counterfeit coins are often cast.
- Circulated: Being circulated is why most of the coins were made (to be handled hand-to-hand.) A coin is said to be circulated when it shows signs of wear and tear.
- Clad Coinage: Coins made of different metals with a central and outer layer. Since 1965, all circulating US half dollars, dimes, dollars, and quarters have been clad.
- Coin Grading: A process by which a coin is assessed, based on its level of wear, meaning how minor or how much the wear is. Knowing more than just the different grading levels will help you in the future to prevent prospective buyers and sellers from ripping you off.
- Collar: A metallic piece that stops the planchet from expanding metal during the minting process.
- Commemorative: A unique coin or medal released or dedicated to honoring a significant individual, event, or place.
- Condition: A coin's bodily or physical state.
- Counterfeit: A forged coin or another piece of money made to deceive people into believing it's real.
- Cull Coin: Many people in the coin-collecting world see cull coins as one person's trash as another's treasure. The majority of these coins' designs are highly damaged, worn out, or have different other hitches.
- Currency: Any money, whether coins or paper money, used as an exchange medium.
- Denomination: The various values of currency.
- Die: An inscribed stamp impressing a design (value, images, and mottos) on a blank metal piece to make a coin. It's a complex stamping tool formed to sustain or survive high pressure. Each die has an image that is minted onto the coins.
- Designer: The artist that makes a coin's design but doesn't necessarily incise the design into a coin die.
- Edge: The external border of a coin, considered the "third side" (not to be mistaken for "rim"). An edge is the rim of a coin, usually containing a series of lettering, reeds, or other decoration.
- Engraver: An artist who forms a clay model of a coin's design in bas release.
- Error: A coin made wrongly during the minting process (maybe a wrong inscription or date), disregarded in the making and distributed into circulation later. Although it's rare for these coins to find their way into circulation.

The Big Book Of Coin Collecting For Beginners | 23

- Encapsulated Coin: A coin that has been validated, graded, and covered in plastic by an autonomous service.
- Exergue: A section of the coin design divided by a line (frequently representing the ground in the design) where a legend is inscribed/positioned.
- Face Value: The amount at which a coin can be exchanged or spent (a dime's face value is .10) compared to its collector or valuable metal worth.
- Field: The background part of a coin's surface without any inscription or design.
- Fleur de coin (FDC): A coin of outstandingly high quality, where quality is not only determined by the wear of the coin in circulation but also by the wear and arty quality of the dies where it was struck. These factors are vital for ancient coins, where variability was more in modern mints.
- Grade: This is the coin condition or the level of wear and tear that a coin has received. Common grade terms used in the UK include Fine, Very Fine, Extremely Fine, and Uncirculated.
- Hairlines: Tiny lines or scrapes on coins, often caused by polishing or cleaning.
- High Relief: This is a coin with an elevated design above the field. Coins minted in high relief usually have issues with details not showing enough and die shorter than a usual or regular lifetime. If the design exceeds the edge, the coin may not be stackable, and the design peak points will wear out very fast.
- Incuse: This is the part of the coin design that is pressed into the surface. It's the opposite of relief.
- Ingot: Metal cast into a specific shape; used in producing coins.
- Inscription: Terms stamped or printed on a coin or medal.
- Intrinsic Value (Bullion Value): Present market worth of the valuable metal in a coin.
- Key Date: A rare date needed to complete a collection, often more challenging to get and afford.
- Laureate: A style of coin photography that began in ancient Rome, usually displaying the emperor's head crowned with a laurel wreath. A recent instance is the first picture of Her Majesty the Queen, inscribed on UK coins from 1953 to 1967.
- Legal Tender: Dollar bills, coins, or other coinage issued as official money by a government.
- Legend: The primary inscription or lettering on a coin.
- LEP: This is the abbreviation of Limited-Edition Presentation—a term that refers to the sets of coins or the number of coins presented in a particular style.
- Lettered Edge: The outer edge of a coin with an inscription.
- Low Relief: A coin with an elevated design that's not that high beyond the field.
- Luster: The ability of a coin's look to reflect brightness and brilliance.
- MCM: An abbreviated term for Maximum Coin Mintage—a term that refers to the highest number of coins that will be released.
- Medal: A metal object similar to a coin issued to commemorate a person or group, place, or event with no specified value or intention to circulate as currency.
- Medium of Exchange: Whatever people agree has a particular value.
- Mint: A place where country coins are produced under the government's authority.
- Milled Edge: Also referred to as a Reeded Edge, this is the coin edge with grooved lines around the perimeter.
- Mint Luster: The frosty, dull, or satiny gloss seen on uncirculated coins.
- Mintmark: A small letter or symbol on a coin specifying the United States Mint facility that minted the coin.
- Mint Set: A comprehensive coin set of each denomination

made by a specific mint.
- Mint State: This also means uncirculated.
- Mintage: The quantity of coins that was manufactured. For instance, a mintage of 1,000 coins.
- Motto: A term, phrase, or sentence printed on a coin to describe a national guiding principle, like E Pluribus Unum, a Latin phrase that means "out of many, one," printed on every US circulating coin.
- Mylar: Trademark for a polyester film that keeps coins.
- Numismatics: A word used to describe the study or collection of coins and money.
- Numismatist: Someone that collects coins.
- Obsolete: A coin type or design that is not produced any longer.
- Obverse: A coin's head or front side.
- Off-Center: This is a term used to describe a coin that has had a misaligned strike from the coin press, and some parts of its design are missing.
- Overstrike: A new coinage made with a minted coin that was used previously as the planchet.
- Pattern: A trial or experimental part of a new design or metal.
- Piedfort: Pronounced "pee a fort," this refers to a coin minted on a planchet that is usually two times thicker than regular.
- Planchet: A disc-shaped metal blank on which the picture of a coin is stamped.
- Proof: A coin explicitly made for a collector from highly polished planchets and dies, usually minted more than once to emphasize the design. Proof coins have the highest quality mint possible and can be distinguished by their frosty foreground and mirror-like surface or background. Other typical characteristics include complex designs with high mints and frosted lettering.
- Proof Set: A collection of proof coins of each denomination produced in a year.
- Relief: Opposite of incuse. This is the part of a coin's design that's elevated beyond the surface.
- Restrike: A coin that is struck with the original die later.
- Reverse: The back or tail side of the coin.
- Riddler: A machine that screens out blanks or planchets that are not the right shape or size.
- Rim: An elevated rim or border on both sides of a coin (made by the upsetting mill) that assists the coin's design from wear and tear. It also makes the coins stackable and easy to roll by machine.
- Roll: Coins packed by dealers, banks, or the US Mint.
- Series: A coin collection comprised of all date and mintmarks of a particular design and denomination.
- Slab: Nickname for some defensive coin encapsulation methods, particularly the ones that are permanently sealed and rectangular. Slabbed Coin is the coin case—a sealed, tamper-evident plastic holder in which an authenticated coin has been housed. If a coin has been validated and graded by a reputable company like PCGS, collectors will see these collector's items as highly valuable. This accounts for the reasons coin collectors love them.
- SOTD: An abbreviation of the term "Strike on the Day." It refers to a dedicatory coin that has been minted on the same day as a significant historic or royal event.
- Strike: The process of engraving a design on a coin blank. The imprint strength—full, average or weak—affects uncommon coins' worth.
- Toning: The surface film triggered by oxidation, typically brown or green, often found on older bronze, copper, or silver coins. Also referred to as "patina," this feature can improve the detail on silver coins, hence enhancing their desirability.
- Truncation: A sharply cut-off lowest edge of an image or bust. The truncation is usually where the coin inscriber's monograms are found.

- Type Set: This refers to a coin collection based on denomination.
- Uncirculated: Also known as Brilliant Uncirculated or Mint Coin. A coin that has never been used, therefore retaining all or most of its actual luster. These coins have very slight, if any, faults or signs of wear. They usually command higher payouts from potential purchasers, so it is essential to maintain them well. Uncirculated coins are made with the same process as circulating coins but with quality improvements like slightly higher coining strength, distinct cleaning after stamping, early strikes from dies, and unique packaging.
- Upsetting Mill: A machine that increases the rim on both sides of a blank (planchet).
- Variety: A slight transformation from the fundamental design of a coin.
- Year Set: A collection of all coins released by a nation for any one year (doesn't have to include all mintmarks).

Overall, this chapter has broadened your knowledge of coin collection, who collects coins, the purpose of coin collection, and the terminology you need to know as a coin collector.

Feeling a bit more prepared to dive into coin collecting now that you have these fundamental terms under your belt? The next chapter has you covered.

It comprehensively covers all you need to know about how to collect coins, including the tools and accessories you need to collect coins, where to find coins for coin collection, and how to identify counterfeit coins.

Chapter 5
How to Collect Coins

Humanity has been attracted to collecting for thousands of years. Whether coins, rocks, shells, books, or tools, item collection awakens our interest and curiosity. Collecting makes time stand still by bringing the past along with us.

We would not know of the past if not for the stories we are told, both orally and documented. However, details and genuineness can be lost as these stories are passed down.

The past comes to life with collectibles. We can remember the past through objects used by people who lived before us. And this was primarily true of coins because they were the means of daily commerce and are still in some places. Coins, whether old or more recent, are historical reminders.

When you come across a coin that is 50 or even 2000 years old, you can't but imagine where it might have been in its lifetime and what it connotes.

Many coin collectors started by finding an exciting coin in their pocket, acquiring a few coins by some other means, or inheriting a coin collection. Others started by thinking they had found a valuable and rare coin, therefore, looking for ways to get rich quickly.

Nevertheless, you will need tips to ensure a long and profitable coin-collecting journey.

How to Get Started with Collecting Coins

Finding your interest is the first step of your journey in coin collecting. For example, you might be interested in a certain period of history or build up a collection of unique edition coins released to commemorate landmark anniversaries and events.

Whichever coin you want to collect, buy a few coin folders to store your collection, so they can keep looking their best. You can purchase blank folders or organized ones by date and type of coin. Having an album makes you ready for hunting coins.

Unsure where to begin? You can also join a community to learn more about your hobby!

Top Expert-Proven Tips for Collecting Coins

START SMALL AND SIMPLE

Unless you are a millionaire and wouldn't mind some financial loss, you should ease into the hobby and learn the ropes before making any significant purchases.

You can start with smaller coin purchases and coin sets that are easy to gather. Learn about the coins, their pricing, their history, and how to grade them. People that became great coin collectors started by assembling a set of Lincoln pennies.

These pennies can still be found in circulation. You can buy them for a moderate price at a local coin show or online.

HANDLE COINS CAREFULLY AND STORE THEM PROPERLY

Since coins are made of metal, many people are not careful when handling them. The surface of a coin is delicate and can easily be damaged. Also, metals react differently with the atmosphere around them.

Practicing handling techniques and safe coin storage will protect the value of your coins for a long time. For instance, you can handle your coin wearing latex or cotton gloves. However, you should hold the coin by its edge if these are unavailable.

In addition, do not clean a coin. Coin dealers can tell when a coin has been cleaned, which can be considered a damaged coin. Cleaning coins can also reduce their value or even make them worthless.

JOIN A COIN CLUB

One of the smartest ways to learn about coins and stay interested in coin collecting is to join a coin club. A quick internet search can help you locate the nearest club in your city or town.

For instance, The American Numismatic Association (ANA) is the most prominent organization in the USA dedicated to numismatic education.

Several specialty coins clubs focus on early American copper coins, error coins, Liberty Seated type coins, etc. No matter the level of your expertise or area of interest, there will always be a coin club that meets your standard.

COLLECT WHAT YOU LIKE:

It is advisable to collect coins that interest you; it may be about a fascinating design on the coin or the story behind it. In addition, you can research the coin's history on the internet to learn about its origin. You should, however, be careful when purchasing coins online to avoid being cheated.

Some collectors collect world coins that have a similar theme, like fish, flowers, buildings, queens, etc. The possibilities are endless and exciting as you make them.

HAVE A PLAN

Before starting a coin collection, you must research the amount required to assemble the collection. You don't have to start a particular collection because it is a showstopper coin. You can save up and wait until you have enough money to buy the more expensive coins.

Setting up a spreadsheet to list the coins you would need to complete a particular collection, their grade, and the estimated cost of each coin, can also help.

DO NOT RUSH

Building a collection of coins that will appreciate with time isn't a race. Those who rush to purchase end up regretting it and lose money when they eventually sell their coin collections. Take time to learn about the coins before buying them.

VISIT A COIN SHOP OR A COIN SHOW

Although you can purchase many coins online, you won't be able to hold, inspect, or compare them. Instead, visiting a local coin shop or coin show will help you evaluate the coin before purchasing it.

A coin dealer can also provide valuable information to help your purchase.

Coin-Collecting Tools and Accessories

Coin collectors need coin-collecting tools and accessories to determine the value of the coins they want to acquire or those they possess. Besides finding defects, tools can help

The Big Book Of Coin Collecting For Beginners | 29

you discover the coin's intrinsic beauty and value.

The minimum tools a numismatist should have is a magnifier and the right reference books. It is also advisable to make an adequate light source available for coin examination. Other tools are required to give more options when examining and admiring a coin.

Proper Storage System

Essential tools such as coin folders, envelopes, holders, or albums are needed to keep your coins safe, organized, and secured. In addition, these tools will protect your coins from a harsh environment and from being exposed to air, thereby preserving their value.

It is advisable to choose a storage that protects your coins from fire or theft and ensures that there would be no scratches or nicks on the coin once inside.

Magnifying Glass

It is essential to have a high-quality magnifying glass to examine the tiny details of a coin. Ensure your magnifier has four to ten times magnification, although most coin collectors prefer seven times magnification.

A low-power magnifier would be your best option to see hairline and other tiny imperfections when examining smaller coins or proof coins. A high-power magnification can overemphasize defects and lead the grader to inconsistent and incorrect grading options.

Based on the Professional Coin Grading Service (PCGS) standard, Mint State 70 coins don't show any defect when you use a five times magnifying glass for examination.

A Journal or Logbook

Creating records like a catalog, journal, or logbook for your collection is an excellent idea. You can keep crucial information about your coin acquisition for insurance and personal use. For instance, you can include the coin types, date, denomination and mint, its state of preservation, and where the coin was struck in your journal.

You can also buy a digital camera to take pictures of coins and add these to your record. This will facilitate downloading and editing of pictures when needed.

Proper Lighting

Proper lighting for your coin goes hand in hand with your magnifying glass. It is recommended to use a 75-watt incandescent light or even higher. However, the actual brightness depends on the available surrounding light.

Some coin collectors prefer to use a halogen lamp. According to those who have used it, halogen light is suitable for detecting hairlines on coins, especially if used to examine proof coins. However, you should be careful because it can strain your eyes if used for too long.

In addition, you shouldn't use white light emitted by fluorescent lights because they don't show the details of a coin.

Nowadays, expert coin dealers and professional collectors use a more expensive type of light. Some use fiber optic lights that give a more concentrated beam of light and consistent color. This light gives a more precise assessment of the coin, whether being checked with the naked eye or under a magnifying glass.

You can also get a magnifier lamp which will supply you with a light source and a magnifier built into one appliance. Although these magnifiers are not optically corrected, the light that illuminates from these units is not as reliable as an independent light source.

The ideal setup for doing your coin examination should be a comfortable location free from any outside distractions. This is vital to help you focus on the task at hand. Distractions can give you wrong assessments and cause you to miss details.

Calipers

Calipers are tools used to measure coins' thickness and diameter accurately within a millimeter. Precise dimensions may aid coin identification, especially for more difficult coins like ancient currencies.

There are different types of calipers, but some of the easiest to use have a digital display.

Digital Scale

One of the major criteria for coin identification is its weight; a digital scale can help with this. In addition, a digital scale is vital because it helps to detect fraudulent coins, which can look real but are composed of different light metals.

These scales are readily available in the market. You can search for a model that accurately measures to at least two decimal places.

Cotton Gloves

Handling expensive and rare coins with your bare hands is not recommended. This is because the oil from your skin might react with the metal and create long-term damage. Instead, you should purchase lint-free cotton gloves to handle your coins because they are nonreactive, soft, and pleasant.

Magnifier

You will need a magnifier to examine coin details closely and frequently. You can purchase a small portable magnifier with a magnification of five to ten for a thorough inspection of your coin. It is small but can be used at coin shows, shops, and even at home.

A loupe can also be a good choice, as it is portable and folds into its case; it is often used by jewelers. Choose the one that you will be most comfortable with.

USB Microscope

A USB microscope is a good investment for professional collectors and dealers looking to deal in higher magnification than a portable magnifier or loupe.

These microscopes are less expensive and more portable compared to traditional microscopes. In addition, they have a mini camera that connects to a computer through USB to take digital close-up photos of your coins with unique details.

This tool would benefit individuals who want to take grading coins professionally and seriously.

Coin Tongs or Tweezers

Using tongs and coin tweezers are good ways to handle valuable and rare coins. These help when greater agility than one gloved hand can give is required—for instance, placing coins into holders or albums or looking at coins closely.

Ensure you buy a tong or tweezer specially made for handling coins because they will have a protective coating at the tips. This coating will prevent your coins from being damaged.

Flat-Clinch Stapler

A flat-clinch stapler is considered the best to staple the cardboard surrounding the coin, using 2x2s to keep it tight and secure. This is because a regular stapler can leave swollen points that can tear the plastic album pages or destroy nearby coins.

Dehumidifier

Water is not ideal for coins because it can make them rust. The key to long-lasting coin storage is to keep coins cool and dry. You can get an automated dehumidifier or add a desiccant packet to your storage to preserve it from rusting.

Locations for Coin Collecting

- The easiest coin collecting method is concentrating on the current circulating ones. However, you might want to branch off into other coins that are out of circulation. You can get excellent resources for information from dealers with their coin stores.
- You can join several coin shows and purchase from various dealers simultaneously to make a better choice.
- Buying via mail. Unfortunately, over-grading or getting problems from specific mail-order sources is too common. Ensure the source has a reasonable return policy before buying. Once you get the coin, thoroughly analyze the coins to guarantee that they are acceptable.
- The most expensive and rarest coins are mostly offered at auctions, promoted by specialized companies, usually in bigger cities. It is not uncommon for bids to go significantly higher or lower than prices during auctions. Check prices in stores, websites, mail-order, and advertisements, to avoid paying an excessive amount.
- You can also purchase or trade from another collector, although finding collectors who offer the exact coin you desire is challenging. However, you might get a more desirable price when it occurs.
- Coin collector message boards can be used to make contacts. Perform a Google search or look around.
- Coins are often offered at flea markets, antique shows, craft fairs, and other occasions where they are not the focal point. However, since there is little or no competition for sellers and prospective buyers are not well-educated about the hobby, you can use these places to move coins.

Types of Fake Coins

CAST COUNTERFEIT COINS

A cheap way to produce fake coins is to create a mold of the real coin and use it to cast a counterfeit. Making the mold is relatively simple. The original coin is used as a model to produce the cast coin.

Counterfeiters use this method because this process does not destroy the original coin. Once the molds have been prepared, the molten metal is poured into them. More skilled counterfeiters use a centrifuge to ensure that the molten metal reaches every part of the cast.

Regardless of the casting technique, a low-quality fake coin is always produced. Also, cast counterfeit coins easily detect counterfeit coins.

STRUCK COUNTERFEITS COINS

Struck counterfeit coins are made the same way a genuine coin is manufactured. This is done by placing a planchet between two coin dies. Then, the Counterfeiter pours the coin dies into a coining press with several tons of pressure used to strike the counterfeit coins.

The counterfeiters can make the coin dies by inscribing them by hand, using spark erosion. They can also use other methods such as one-to-one transfer engraving lathes, the plating technique, or the impact method. Unfortunately, any of these methods lead to a deceptive counterfeit coin.

This process is the most tedious and costly way to create a counterfeit coin. That is why only the more valuable coins are counterfeited using the struck fake method.

DOCTORED AND ALTERED COUNTERFEIT COINS

The cheapest and quickest way to make money in coin counterfeit production is to take a regular coin and modify it to look like an expensive and rare coin. For example, a counterfeiter can purchase a 1909 Lincoln Cent with the designer's initials of VDB on the reverse for under $20. A skilled counterfeiter can add an S mintmark to the obverse, making the coin appear worth more.

Another method of altering the coin is eliminating slight details to improve the coin's worthiness. For instance, an unscrupulous person with no experience can remove the S mintmark on a 1928-S Peace Dollar, which can easily increase the coin's value tenfold.

Split coins are another example of a fake coin that has been radically plagiarized. The counterfeiter will take two popular coins, divide them in half, and solder the two halves together. This process will yield a coin that gives the illusion of a rare and more costly coin.

For instance, a Buffalo Nickel minted in 1926 at the Philadelphia Mint can be sold for under $100. Another model minted in 1929 at the San Francisco Mint can also be purchased for under $100.

A skilled counterfeiter can split the two coins in half, use the obverse of the 1926 nickel with the reverse of the 1929 nickel from San Francisco, and create a 1926-S Buffalo Nickel worth close to $10,000.

How to Identify Fake Coins

A fake coin is any coin produced by any person without the knowledge and consent of the issuing country or entity. Regular coins can also be altered to look like expensive coins. Although this might not be fake, it can be considered deception.

An essential skill set to detect fake coins would save you from loss by avoiding the purchase of counterfeit coins. However, if you want to invest substantial money in coins, it is best to protect yourself by getting familiar with the best ways to identify counterfeit coins.

Locate the Seam

Fake coins have casting seams which can be very obvious to the naked eye. Frequently, counterfeit coins have hole markings. In addition, many coins have complex textures

The Big Book Of Coin Collecting For Beginners | 33

and designs that are common with that particular coin and its series. If you suspect something is inconsistent, it is best to inquire elsewhere.

Study the Markings

Frequently, counterfeit coins do not have mintmarks consistent with a certified coin. In such cases, ensure you do enough research about the marks and designs that are consistent with the piece you want to buy. Once you have inspected the gold or silver coin, you can ask if the seller has paperwork to back up their claim of the coin if certain marks are missing or do not add up.

It Should Melt

Silver is a heat conductor, so it immediately emits thermal energy to melt an ice cube without assistance. Therefore, if your silver coin doesn't begin the melting process immediately after it is placed on an ice cube, then the odds are that it is not authentic.

Find the Relief

Counterfeiters find it hard to get the relief of a coin just right. Usually, they are either too low or high. A potential buyer can test the coin's originality by saving it with coins from the same series. However, you must be more cautious with the transaction if the stack falls over.

Opposites Attract

Magnets do not attract elements such as silver or gold. Consequently, if your coin collection is attracted to the magnet, then it is most likely not genuine.

Chapter 6
How to Preserve, Store, and Protect your Collection

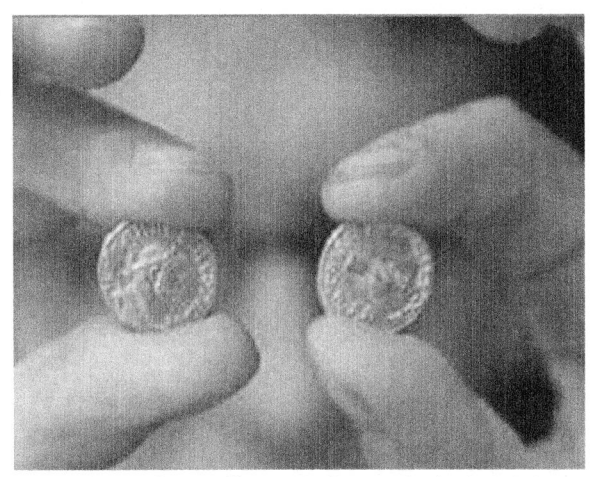

The passage of time affects all things, coins included. Some effects can be conspicuous such as design details worn away by circulation or surfaces marred by contact with other coins. Although these effects can be less obvious, it doesn't make it less critical; coins need protection after they become part of your collection.

The stealthy effects of exposure to the atmosphere can alter a coin's appearance with time, making prized pieces a shadow of their former self. However, you can preserve your collection by following some thoughtful steps and a modest expenditure on storage.

How to Handle your Coin Correctly

Avoid Handling Your Coin Roughly

Contact through the skin or touching coins with your bare hands can damage your coin. Although it cannot be seen with the naked eye, the human skin secrets oils and acids, and touching your coin with naked fingers can leave these deposits on their surface, thereby eventually causing damage to them.

Hold Coin Properly

There are ways you should hold coins. First, ensure that you hold them by the edges, between your forefingers and thumb, to avoid touching the face of the coin. You should also hold a coin over a soft place if it falls. This is to avoid scratches on a hard surface.

Clean with Mild Soap or Water

When cleaning a coin to remove dirt, use only mild soap and clean water and dry it with a towel. However, some experts advise that coins are not cleaned or polished to keep their value. This is because improper cleaning to make coins look shiny can devalue them.

Hence, if the coin does not have dirt that needs to be cleaned, it is unnecessary to clean them to keep them in the same condition you found them. In addition, an old coin with deep age coloration has more value and is more desirable than a polished one, with surface scratches appearing new.

Use a Protective Holder

Collectors' coins should be handled carefully to avoid wear or the introduction of substances that could cause color changes or spots. Many holders provide enough protection for normal handling but are careful before removing a coin from its holder. Only uncirculated coins or the edge of proofs should be touched because even fingerprints can potentially reduce the grade and value of the coin.

Once your coin is outside a holder, place it on a clean, soft surface. An ideal surface is a velvet pad for handling valuable materials regularly. Also, a blank piece of paper or a clean, soft cloth can suffice for less valuable items. Also, ensure that you don't drag your coin across any surface.

Hold Coin at the Edge

You must ensure that you hold the edge when handling or inspecting another person's coins, regardless of the grade. If you make it a practice, picking up collectible coins by the edge will become second nature.
It is not advisable to hold numismatic objects in front of your mouth because small particles of moisture can cause spots. Also, avoid sneezing or coughing near coins because this can leave marks on the coin and ruin it.

Wear Surgical Gloves and a Face Mask

When handling a precious coin or many higher grades

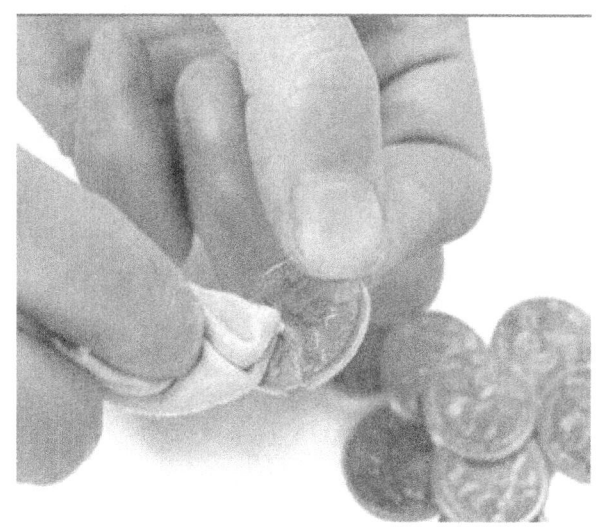

circulated or uncirculated coins, ensure you wear surgical gloves, a mask, or a clean white cloth. Always handle coins with freshly washed cotton gloves.

Another important rule is to avoid causing wear or introducing substances that may cause spots or color changes. Ensure that coins are not touching each other because this can result in nicks and scratches. Take coins out of their storage containers only when necessary to avoid destroying them.

How to Store your Coin

You must store your coins properly to avoid giving them any scratches that can reduce their value. Depending on the value of the coin you are storing, you need to store your coins properly. Folders and albums are available commercially that you can buy to store your series or type of collection.

These tips will help you store your coins more appropriately:

1. When using a paper envelope, ensure that the materials are suitable for holding coins, especially high-value ones. This is because sulfur or other chemicals in the paper causes a reaction and changes the color of the coin.
2. Another good option for long-term storage is plastic flips made of acetate and mylar. These plastic flips are hard and brittle, though they may scratch the coin if not inserted carefully.
3. Tubes are suitable for bulk storage of circulated coins, handle higher-grade coins if not moved, and can hold many same-size coins. However, you should use hard plastic for more valuable coins because they do not contain harmful materials. Also, they protect coins from scratches and other physical damage.
4. Slabs are also a good option for more valuable coins, as they offer protection. They are hermetically sealed rigid plastic holders for each coin. However, slabs are expensive, and you will not be able to get at the coin quickly.
5. A dry environment with low humidity and no significant temperature fluctuation is essential for long-term storage. Minimizing exposure to moist air is good because this can cause oxidation.
6. Although this might not reduce the coin's value, minimal oxidation will help the coin look more attractive. In addition, lace silica gel packets in the coin storage are suitable for controlling atmosphere moisture.
7. You should check on your collection periodically, even when safely stored in a safety deposit box. Then, you can detect early on if your valuables are not stored properly. Also, you can do something about it before severe damage occurs.
8. Avoid extremes such as attics and cellars to maintain your coin collection in the best possible shape. Instead, a den or your bedroom are good options. In addition, choose a place away from the kitchen where moisture and cooking oils will not infiltrate your coin holders and albums.
9. If you are staying near water or the sea, you should take extra steps to protect your coins from damage caused by damp and salty climates. Notably, copper coins are vulnerable to environmental degradation caused by moisture and salt in the air.
10. You can also use a safe deposit box at a bank to keep your coin. However, this can be very expensive. Bank vaults are composed of a substance that emits water vapor to keep the temperature low during a fire outbreak. They are also strongly built to keep criminals away. This is why they are expensive. However, they are one of the safest places to keep your coins and other valuables.
11. You can also buy a safe for your home or business to store your coin since this will save you money. There will be no need to renew the annual cost with a safe

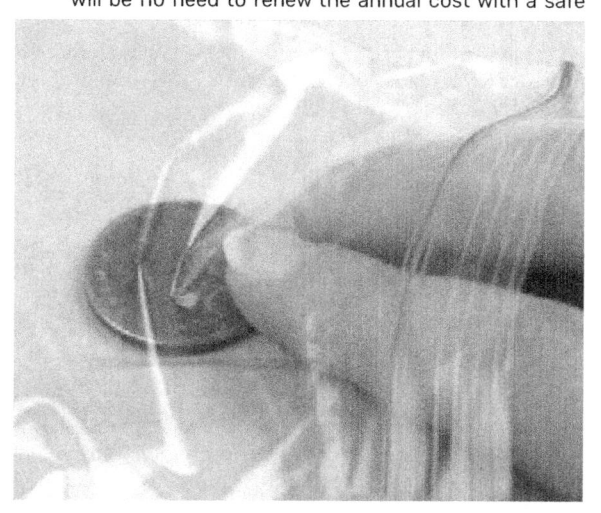

in your home instead of using a bank in the bank. You might also consider buying an alarm system that will help you safeguard your valuables.

12. You can also keep your collectibles in a lockable metal cabinet. Although, they are made with glue, coatings, and wood and can emit dangerous chemicals into your coin collection as they age. Metals have been known to draw moisture when they condense, so you must be careful where you put your metal cabinet.

Causes of Coin Damage

Extremely High or Low Collection
Storing your coins in too-warm places can cause air pollution and acid and increase moisture, damaging the coins faster than expected. Similarly, keeping your coin in an area with a low temperature can lead to condensation on the coin's surface.

Humidity

This is the most common cause of damage in collectible coins since copper and silver cause chemical reactions with moisture which can occur anywhere. For this reason, it can be difficult to reduce the risk.

Acids

You don't have to pour acids on your coins before it damages them. Some coin holders and storage supplies are made from cardboard and paper, and acids are commonly found in these materials. Therefore, using these materials can tone or tarnish the coin.

Air Pollution

It is not only humans that air pollution is dangerous for; it can also be detrimental to coins. Therefore, you should protect your coins by keeping them away from the air as much as possible, if you can, especially if you stay around a metropolitan area.

Chlorine

Chlorine is a harsh chemical that can corrode coins and lead to toning. However, it isn't only when you dip your coin in chlorine that you can see this effect. Some plastic coin holders contain PVC, which consists of a chlorine composition. Therefore, it is crucial to use PVC-free coin holders.

Rough Handling

You should be extremely careful when handling your coin, as any lousy handling can cause significant damage to your valuables. In addition, it is advisable to hold your coin by the edges to avoid destroying or devaluating it. The more you protect your coin, the higher the probability of surviving the sands of time, and they can appreciate with time.

How to Take Care of Collectible Coins

If you want to display your coins, you shouldn't keep them on a high, unstable shelf because they might fall over. However, you can use a two-pocket box made of polyester since they are made explicitly for storing coins.

In addition, coins can gather dirt over time. You can adopt several strategies to clean your coin. However, it would help if you didn't wash your coins because this can devalue them. It is also advisable to wear a mask while holding your coin. Although wearing a mask is not strictly necessary, spit from your mouth can get to the coin, affecting it.

Storing your coin in an airtight container with decontaminated water and sand is easy to clean. And to brighten your valuables, seal the container and shake it firmly. However, doing this depends on abrasion, so it is not recommended for ancient and precious coins.

You should always seek the advice of a reputable coin grading service before cleaning your collectible coins. A proper way to clean your coin without washing it is to use a cotton swab and apply Vaseline or other lubricants on this swab. Then, dab the coin gently with a specialized lint-free cloth to remove the Vaseline.

This technique will help you remove the dirt on the coin without affecting its value. However, you should use a magnifying glass with caution when you use this method. Also, you can apply the Vaseline using a delicate non-synthetic brush or a g-tip. However, you should avoid using too much Vaseline on the coin because this can also affect the value of the coin.

Another method is to dip the coin in acetone for five seconds. Then, applying methanol to your coin can make it a bit brownish and reduce its value. For this reason, you shouldn't keep it in the solution for too long. Instead, you should rinse immediately with distilled water after you remove it from the acetone and then air dry it.

Acetone is a solution, not an acid, so it will not affect your coin or devalue it until it is exposed for a prolonged time. You should also know that this solution is flammable, so wear powder-free gloves. Line the bottom of the distilled water jar you want to use with a napkin so that your coins won't sustain scratches when they touch each other in the jar.

It is also advisable to only use 100% pure acetone because anything less than that can devalue your valuable.

- How to Clean Different Types of Coins

    1. Gold Coins: You should be extra careful when cleaning gold coins to avoid scratching or disfiguring them. They should be cleaned carefully in a clean, lukewarm, purified liquid using a soft toothbrush or cottony fiber wash-down fabric.
    2. Uncirculated Coins: This type of coin should never be cleaned because it can ruin its mint luster.
    3. Copper Coins: To clean them, copper coins should be soaked in grape oil. However, you should avoid rubbing them together because this can affect their value. Also, it takes several weeks to see the result, so you must be patient.
    4. Nickel Coins: The best way to clean nickel coins is by using warm, soapy, distilled water and a soft toothbrush. However, if you notice that you have damaged the coin while cleaning it, then you can use ammonia diluted with distilled water to correct that.
    5. Silver Coins: Just like uncirculated coins, silver coins should never be cleaned. In fact, dirt and residue can enhance the coins and add value to them. However, dark silver coins can be cleaned using alcohol, ammonia, vinegar, or polish remover with acetone.

PROTECTING YOUR COIN COLLECTION FROM LOSS BY THEFT OR FIRE

There will always be a threat of loss by theft or fire to any property. Nevertheless, there are some precautions you should put in place to protect your coin, just as you would protect your house or car.

You should know that most homeowners don't have insurance that covers coins or other numismatic items. However, you can acquire a separate policy that covers your coin. Some associations, such as the American Numismatic Association (ANA), offer insurance for coin collections for their members.

It will help if you keep a collection catalog separate from the coins (the catalog should contain where you bought the coin, the price, and the condition). Another thing you should do is take pictures of each coin in the of case any unfortunate event.

Safes can protect your valuables from fire, theft, water, dust, etc., that could destroy your possessions. You should know that some of these safes are not versatile. For instance, some protect your collection from fire but are unsuitable for theft, while some can keep thieves away but not fire. Even if the flames do not touch your coins, your valuables can be destroyed by fire heat.

Another thing you should also consider is the humidity level. A high-level humidity can cause oxidation which is not good for your collections. The proper humidity level for your coin is 30%.

The ambient Relative Humidity (RH) inside the safe is

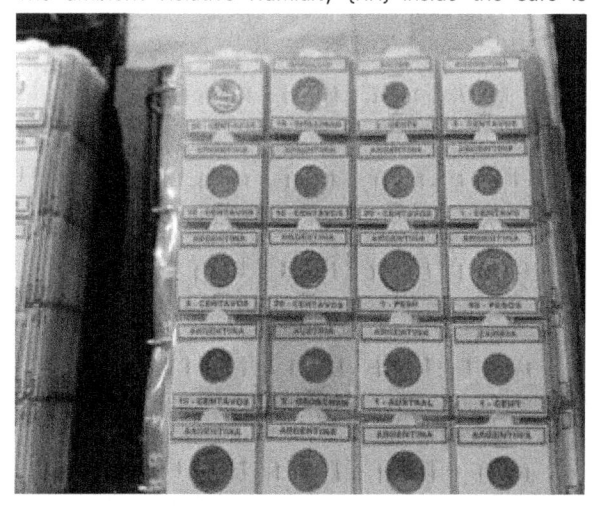

before making a purchase. You can check prices from reliable coin periodicals or sight-unseen exchange networks to ensure you are not overpaying.

When comparing prices, you can easily find out if a dealer is selling you a counterfeit coin. If the price the seller gives you is significantly lower than other resources, the grade or quality might also be low.

You should also be careful when giving credit card information, especially over the phone. If the seller gives high-pressure sales techniques, that is another reason not to buy. This is because most sellers with this sales attitude are not authentic.

determined by the RH of where it is located. However, most safes are insulated and constructed with good seals, and the silica gel can also reduce humidity.

Thus, if you decide to keep your collection at home, ensure that you get a safe that can protect your coins from both fire and theft. Ensure that you also take other measures to dissuade thieves from your house. For instance, your home should have adequate lighting and strong locks.
You should also be discreet about being a coin collector or having your valuables at home. Divulging sensitive information about yourself to many people can eventually get to the wrong person and make both you and your home a target.

How to Avoid Rare Coin Scam

You should use your good judgment when analyzing claims; don't be in a hurry to buy. Instead, probe the dealer's dependability and standing when you want to buy. Also, try to find out how long the seller has been in the coin-collecting business and contact the professional group the vendor is under for claim validity.

You should stay away from brokers that promise to repurchase your coins at the price you paid for them at a later time. Get a second assessment on the grade and value of the coins immediately after the broker receives your coins.

Also, if the second view is different, inquire which treatments the seller has to offer before you buy. For example, will you be given a complete refund or credit when you purchase additional coins?

It is advisable to compare prices from different vendors

Chapter 7
Selling your Coin

Coin collecting is profitable for people who do it the right way. Interestingly, there are many ways to sell your coin online, and there's no right or wrong method. However, before selling your coin, there are some tips you must understand to avoid pitfalls.

Tips for Selling Coins

Selling your coin can be somewhat challenging, especially with the various associated factors and strategies you must consider. These strategies include, but are not limited to, employing the proper marketing technique, posting accurate sales ads, and accurate coin grading.

For better understanding, I have carefully examined a few more tips you must consider while selling your coin.

1. Don't Clean Your Coins: Unlike selling a car or other related items, you do not need to clean your coin before selling. Many think cleaning their coins makes them look neat and valuable, but this idea is invalid.
2. Know What You Have: Some people sell their coins not because they are interested in selling them but because they inherited them and didn't want to waste them. Therefore, they lack knowledge about handling them, which is a significant disadvantage to the seller. If you want to make good sales in selling your coin, you should be knowledgeable about handling it.
3. Don't Sell Your Coin Out of Desperation: Take your time to know accurately how, when, and where to sell your coin. The more knowledge you gain about the coin industry, the better off you'll be during sales. Also, don't sell coins because you need urgent money; it might not be the right time to sell.
4. Find the Approximate Value of Your Coins: Know what your coin is worth before you sell, but before doing this, remember that most coin price guides give you a retail value. So if you are buying at retail prices, don't expect to receive the prices listed in the guides.
5. If you are buying from a dealer, the retail value is how much your coins are worth. The amount you'll earn for selling your coins could range from 20% to 50%, depending on the coin type and its condition. If your coin is in poor condition, it may be less valuable.
6. Take Precautions When Trying to Sell: Some precautions are necessary before selling your coins because they guarantee your safety. When you are with your coins, ensure no one is following—many dealers have been robbed by robbers who trailed them.
7. Keep your transactions discreet. If you are shipping your coins, don't use words like "bullion," "gold," or "silver" on the parcel envelopes; it might attract thieves to steal them.
8. Get a Fix on Current Bullion Prices: If you are selling coins, you will likely receive an offer pegged around the spot metal of your material. The spot price is the melt value of the bullion metal in your coins.
9. Find the Right Tools: If you are confident in your expertise, you'll need to purchase tools that will allow you to determine a coin's authenticity on your own. These tools include calipers, a stereo microscope, digital scales, and a daylight lamp.
10. Shop Around: Once you know how much your coins might be worth, there will be many offers, so take your collection to different dealers instead of going with the first offer. Be careful not to sell your coin to untrustworthy dealers, so you won't lose your coin.

Top Seven Places to Sell your Coins Easily

Identify Your Coins

5. **Shape of the Coin**: Minted coins before the late 1700s have an irregular shape. For example, those printed from 1037 to 1967 have more of a polygon shape, very similar to a circle.
6. Type: This refers to the design of each denomination and not necessarily the type of coin. The type of coin depends on the currency and country of origin.

Now that you know your coin's worth, it's time to understand how to sell it. You need to know what you expect when you sell your coins; whether you want to sell them yourself or give them out to someone, you need to decide and prepare to make the sale.

Though there are many options for selling your coins, with the methods we'll discuss in this chapter, you will understand which works for you. Furthermore, with these methods, you may not have to leave your bed before you can sell.

Coin Shops

To start with, you can sell your coins at a local coin shop. To get one, research local coin shops in your region online and check their customers' reviews and feedback to be sure of the shop's offer.

Check if they'll be interested in the kind of coin you are selling; some dealers would indicate the type of coins they want on their website, then you can select your preference. Most dealers are more likely to buy coins at a fair price, so ensure your price is not too high to chase them away from buying your coin.

When you visit the local shop, and they make an offer to you, try to tell the owner to give you some time to think about it. It would help if you were not too fast to sell because you have visited local shops and already have their prices. So you will go for the one that can afford your price.

Before you learn where to sell your coins, you must first understand such coins' value. And to achieve this, you need to identify those coins.

As discussed earlier in this guide, identifying your coin helps you to know its worth and gives you knowledge of the detailed history of the coin. Remember, because a coin has the words the "United States" on it doesn't mean it's the official US coin; thus, it is necessary to identify the worth of your coin before selling it out.

How to Identify your Coin

Here are top tips to help you identify your coin:

1. The Coin Date: Some collectors prefer to collect coins only by their dates of issuance. For instance, you could prefer to collect coins issued in the 1800s. The year is usually marked on the head side of a coin, but sometimes it's on the reverse.
2. Date and Mintmark Combination: You must understand that collecting coins by dates and mintmarks may be more expensive than just collecting by dates. This is because some coin series have a pricey mintmark. Although this does not apply to all coins, you could collect some at a lower price.
3. Denomination: Every currency has different denominations. For instance, the United States currency has the penny, the nickel, the dime, the quarter, the half dollar, and the dollar. So if you want to go big, you may choose the oldest denomination.
4. **Language**: To identify your coin, check the coin language or text; it will give you more information about its region or origin. For example, if you can understand the language, the coin might be from your region or nearby.

value fees are based upon the final selling of an item, so select with care what coins you want to sell on eBay. When listing your coin on eBay, use high-quality images and competitive prices to make your product stand out from other sellers. Remember that eBay charges a percent of your sales.

HOW TO USE EBAY

If you are new to eBay and you are interested in using their marketplace to sell your coin, it's as simple as 1-2-3; here are some tips to guide you:

1. Understanding How eBay Works: eBay is a marketplace that charges the seller a fee for listing products on its platform. The fee includes the listing fees and final value fees. eBay may allow you to list over 200 products for free; however, you will pay a percentage of the sales price, and a token of tax would be demanded if required by law.
2. Start Simple: As a starter on eBay, begin with low-cost coins that people would love to buy. Start with any coin with a value between $5 and $15 because if you make any mistake, your loss won't be significant. Using this strategy would help you progress into selling more expensive coins.
3. Know the Coin's Value: Knowing the value of your coin is important when selling your coins on eBay. You need to identify the coin to get an approximate value of its wholesale price.
4. Quality Pictures: The best way to attract more buyers to your coin on eBay is by using high-quality and accurate pictures. Poor-quality pictures make your coin look blurry and unattractive to your buyers, so use high-quality cameras to take photos before listing it on eBay.

Contrarily, to sell your coin immediately, you will get an instant markdown on the price offered. You may find using a local shop disadvantageous because you may not get the best price for your coins there.

Auctions

You can decide to submit your coins to auctions. Submitting your coins for auction can be done either locally, regionally, or nationally and can happen online or physically.

A great way to sell coins is through specialist and general online auctions, especially if your business targets other collections.

You can try online auctions with a large flow of sellers and products; they charge large commissions for each closed deal. Some big platforms include Heritage Auction Galleries, Goldberg Coins, USA Coin Booke, etc.

Selling your coin on auction increases the likelihood of sales on auction day. Sometimes, your coin may not meet the reserve and may not sell, but the method would help you shift stock quickly.

eBay

Selling coins on eBay is not difficult. On eBay, you can effortlessly introduce your coins to both existing customers and potential buyers. But to start with, you'll need to create an accurate eBay listing!

eBay listing is not free; shipping fees, listing fees, and final

Coin Shows

At the coin show, you have the opportunity of meeting hundreds of dealers at the same time. Therefore, you can make huge offers, depending on the buyers attending the show and how you communicate with them. Then, once you've received some offers, you can choose your buyer.

This method would yield higher than selling directly to a local dealer, but it can be discouraged if you fear traveling to far places.

Your Website

Although the methods mentioned earlier are helpful, having your website would position you for influence as a coin seller. How can you go about this method?

Create your online store for selling your coins. With your website, you have full control of your sales, which would yield more profit. You can also collect emails to run campaigns, social media advertisements, and Google adverts without commissions.

Your website provides secure transactions about your coins, and you can sync it to eBay and Amazon.

Coin Dealer

Selling to coin dealers can be lucrative if you know how to pick up coins below market value. It's simple; take the coin to the dealer and bargain about the price you both are willing to accept. Of course, they would likely bargain your offer for less than what you want to sell it, but you need to stand firm if the price is not convenient for you.

Bullion Dealers

Another option to sell your coin is using bullion dealers, especially when selling bullion and slabbed coins. However, online bullion dealers mostly deal with large orders and refuse to purchase coins less than $1,000.

Amazon

Amazon is an alternative to eBay; it has the largest audience of customers and is meant not only for private but also for primary sellers.

Smelters and Refiners

You can visit a smelter or refinery if you want to melt your coin for its precious metal. Of course, this is only recommended when the coin does not pose much value, but you still want to profit by melting its precious metal.

To a Pawnshop

A pawn shop might be willing to buy your coin depending on the coin and its rarity, though the price might be lower than the market price because the pawn shop still has to make a profit from the deal.

On Forums and Social Media Platforms

Social media gives you access to connect with different groups and forums interested in coin collection. Providing the necessary documentation of your coin is required to boost people's interest on these platforms.

Top Mistakes to Avoid when Selling your Coins

Coin collection can be fun but frustrating if you don't understand the strategies and the mistakes to avoid.

Collecting Coins to Make Money

It is not advisable to venture into the coin collection business because you need money. Newbies in coin collection usually have this mindset; they claim that every coin investment would increase in value. Truthfully, making money from coin collection can take a long time.

You will miss out on the enjoyment of collecting coins if your purpose is only to make money. Some coins will be worth more money in the future and become volatile. Therefore, it is important to understand how the coin market works. You can do this by joining a digital coin-collecting community where you'll learn from people's life stories.

Not Setting Coin-Collecting Goals

Collecting different types of coins without setting a goal to guide you will put you at risk. Setting a goal makes it easier to know the type of coins that interest you and gives the direction of what you want to achieve.

For example, if your goal is to collect coins from different parts of the world, the goal would be a map that will direct you to find more reasons to attend coin-collecting events where you'll have access to more dealers.

Mishandling Your Coins

There is a proper way to touch your coins for inspection and general viewing purposes. Although, this is permitted to only raw coins because coins in slabs and capsules are already protected. Dealing with raw coins requires proper handling.

Reluctance to Spend Money on Interesting Coins

Although paying too much for coins is not logical, it is not good not to purchase interesting coins because you don't want to be scammed. To avoid being scammed, you should research before buying any coin.

For example, if a certain coin has a book value of $25, and you can only find it for $30. If you ignore buying it because it is overvalued, you may miss the chance to buy it at that value again. Price research for your coins can be done by looking at sold listings on eBay.

Poor Storage Conditions

Your collection's worth is greatly determined by the storage method and location you choose. Your coins can be damaged by moisture and high and low temperatures, so attics and basements are poor choices. Coins should rather be stored in a dry place with a constant, moderate temperature.

The best locations are a personal safe in your home or a bank deposit box. You can put some silica gel packets in your safe or safety deposit box. Organizing your coins is necessary, though it can sometimes be difficult, especially if you enjoy taking coins out.

Organized coins help you identify if the coin is lost or stolen. You can also label them to sell appropriately to the coin value. Proper storage of your coins would prevent them from getting tarnished and avoid scratches affecting a coin's value.

Selling too quickly

Avoid being in haste when it's time to sell an individual coin or the whole collection; be patient and pay attention to the process. Patience could be profitable.

Investing Much in a New Type of Coin

Coin collection requires time to learn. Therefore, before you consider selling a coin, take your time to learn about the type. For instance, if you are collecting Barber Dimes, you must know the price and how difficult it will be to acquire the key dates.

Conducting Minimal Research

Conducting research is vital before selling your coin. You should expand your understanding as you develop more than an interest in coin collection. Research helps you get better prices and learn more about buying and selling the coin.

Following Random Tips

The internet is a place that accepts much information, either good or bad, so not every piece of information you see on the internet is true, and not every tip you see on TV is valid. Following random tips is one mistake some coin sellers make, and it's advisable to avoid it by following valid tips with a realistic foundation that can be proven with facts.

Selling Your Coins: When Is the Best Time?

When is the ideal time to sell your coins? Of course, as a coin collector, several reasons may influence your decision to sell your coin collection. However, whatever the reasons, the truth is that one day, the collector will begin his coin collection sale. The best thing is to know when to sell and when not to.

As we've discussed earlier in this chapter, selling your coins is a means of generating income, and no collectors will want to sell their coins at the wrong time. However, it can be challenging to sell your coin collection if you don't have an idea of how the process works.

To get the most profit from your coin collection sales, you must have patience and the proper knowledge needed to sell your coin at the right time. This process requires more time and research.

Five Questions to Ask to Know the Perfect Time to Sell

DO YOU HAVE FINANCIAL CONSTRAINTS?

If you need a cash flow, need to pay your rent or get some urgent resources, then you can consider your coin collection. It is better to solve your urgent needs and pay your rent than stock up your coins with no income. Financial emergencies always take priority over numismatic wants or needs.

Can You Let Your Coins Go?

Let's say you don't have financial constraints and are still considering selling your coin collection. What's holding up the decision to sell? Maybe you are waiting for the marketplace conditions to be favorable. What if the value of the coin is decreasing? Ask if you are comfortable parting with your coin.

If your answer is no, then when? Determine what you will need to make the necessary move.

The truth is that only you can decide what coins to sell and when to sell them. However, answering these questions and checking other considerations will help you decide when to sell your coins.

Factors that Determine the Perfect Time to Sell

A few collectors sell their coins for different reasons. When a seller has chosen to sell his coins, he should reconsider if it is the perfect time to sell them. He should consider the coin's value and know if the coin will progress nicely or if he will profit by selling the coin.

There are different alternatives a collector could figure out to sell his coins; he might need to sell the coins at the swaps. There is a higher possibility of selling the coin at a greater expense since barters incorporate offering forms, particularly if the coin has a higher worth. Here are several factors that will determine the perfect time to sell your coin collection:

The Type of Coins in the Collection

Different types of coins can make your collection more attractive or less attractive in terms of sales. For example, you can easily be attracted to silver dollars and common/obsolete foreign coins. Silver dollars are available with proof and are among the most collected coins in the world.

Gold and Silver Spot Price

If your coin collection has gold and silver, then the value of

Need Cash to Purchase a Once-in-a-Lifetime Item?

Many collectors sell coins to buy more coins; sometimes, they sell coins they no longer want. But what happens if the coin they intend to buy comes across the block suddenly? Can you be patient until it's resolved? It might take time to sell the coins you no longer need to finance your dream coin before it slips away.

What May Happen If You Wait to Sell?

This is a question many coin collectors ponder when contemplating when to sell their coins. What will the marketplace look like in a few months? What will be the buyer's mood in the next month or a year?

Will you lose an excellent opportunity to sell your coins if you wait to sell? What if personal considerations influence the decision to sell? If you want to wait before selling your coin, won't it affect you? What if you wait for a long time, and you miss out on some opportunity that will make you more profit in selling off your coin? Consider these things and know the best move you should take.

Do You Think You Might Regret Selling Your Coins?

Some coin collectors feel regret when they want to sell their coins. It is an emotion likely associated with selling a unique item that can't be replicated. So think twice before selling your coin, so you won't end in tears. If you don't foresee any issues liquidating it, move to sell when the time is right.

gold and silver can be a significant factor. This is because gold and silver are traded at a higher price, making the market an excellent opportunity to sell at a high point versus a lower one.

Coin Collecting Is Not a "Forever" Hobby

You should often ask yourself, "If I hold on to this coin, will it appreciate?" If you think it won't, then it might be the right time to sell it off.

Thankfully, coin collecting has been made easier with the internet now. eBay has made a great impact for coins by providing a marketplace to sell them.

The Desire for the Collection

Most people who inherit coins find coin collecting uninteresting to them. Especially when the collection size is large, they start thinking of how to store, protect and transport them. Thus, without having a desire for coin collection, you may not be interested in doing a coin-selling business.

The Desire for the Funds vs. the Desire for the Coins

Issues happen in life, and some other circumstances determine whether you should hold or sell your coins.

Frequently Asked Questions About Selling your Coins

Should You Clean Your Coin Before Selling?

The simple answer is NO! when you clean your coin, it will have an altered appearance. You shouldn't attempt to clean your coin because it will lose its value after being cleaned. The truth is that most experienced numismatists can easily spot a cleaned coin.

If your coin is corroded and looks unrecognizable, you may try a solution of mild dish soap and distilled water. Be sure to rinse the coin with distilled water and allow it to dry or give it to a professional to handle the cleaning.

I LOVE COIN COLLECTION, BUT WHERE DO I BEGIN?

First, understand that coin collecting is a hobby, and as a hobby, you must develop an interest in it to enjoy the whole process. There are many ways to start coin collecting. If you are interested in collecting United States coins, reach out to an experienced numismatist to put you through.

I Inherited a Coin Collection. I Don't Know About the Coin Collection, but I Want to Sell Them. How Do I Find a Trusted Buyer?

Trying to sell coins without having background knowledge can be frustrating. You must first learn the approximate value of your coins before attempting to sell them. Several strategies to sell your collection include selling to a dealer or on the internet.

Whichever strategy you choose, you must be an informed seller because once you've agreed to the price, the transaction is final.

WHY SHOULD I KEEP TRACK OF MY COINS?

You need to keep track of your coins because it will help you have a detailed report of coin-collecting transactions.

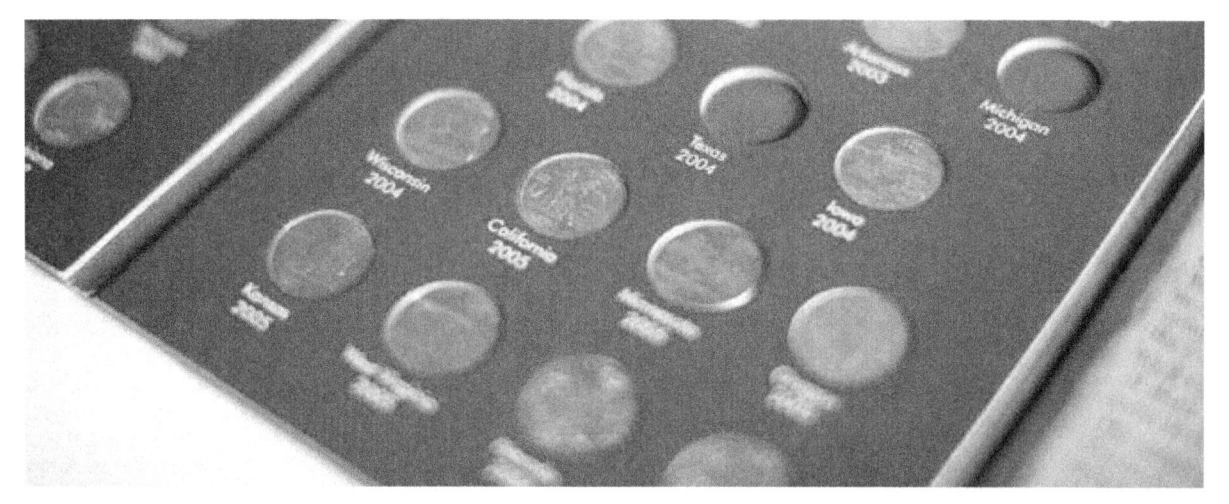

Your coin catalog includes the date of purchase, purchase price, and who sold the collection to you. Also, keeping track of your coins lets you know your coins' value and saves you from the stress of selling when it's not the right time.

HOW DO I KNOW IF A COIN I BUY ONLINE IS LEGIT?

Knowing how the coin-collecting business works, you must be able to view high-resolution images of the coins you are interested in buying. A high-resolution image lets you view the coin's edge, obverse, and reverse. In addition, it is essential to ask your seller tangible questions about the coin you are buying. The seller will disclose all specifications, including the coin's country of origin, mintage, and conditions.

HOW SHOULD I HANDLE MY COINS?

You should handle your coins by the edge, don't try to touch the face of the coin.

WHAT MAKES A COIN VALUABLE?

Supply and demand make a coin valuable. A coin's value is determined by how many are available and the demand for the coin. The market worth will decrease if a particular coin has a high mintage, and people are not after the item.

WHY IS COIN COLLECTING SO POPULAR?

Coin collecting has become even more popular than before because new coins today are connected to historical moments.

WHAT ARE THE BEST RESOURCES FOR COIN COLLECTORS?

One of the best resources for coin collectors is the Red Book. This book is considered to be the numismatist Bible.

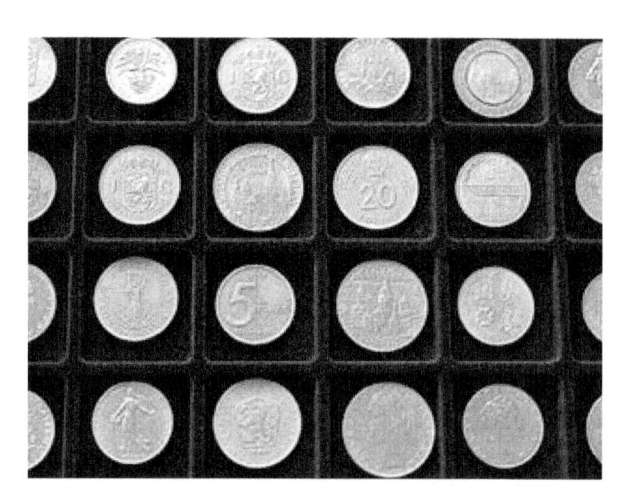

Also, a critical resource for coin collectors is the mentors and friends you connect with at the local coin club. These mentors are experienced and will provide you with a wealth of knowledge in your coin-collecting journey.

Chapter 8
Buying A Coin

Successful coin collectors invest considerable energy into learning almost everything possible about numismatics. They spend more time reading newspapers and magazines and talking to brokers that can provide more information and news about coin collection.

Utilizing any knowledge gained from these excellent sources will help you move before new collectors with the same desire to receive such information.

However, if you decide to start without learning the fundamentals, you may fail miserably. You have to understand how to grade coins because it will help you, as a collector, to determine your collection's actual value. Having information about coin collection will help you identify which coin is worth exchanging with another.

It will also help prevent scams and spending money on something of low value. Always be on the lookout to learn how to run your coin collection business because it might take years to complete if patience is not considered. Many world collectors have waited to reap the benefits of their businesses, and it is paying off today.

Coin collection is similar to sports because it takes time to master and requires you to have some smart goals which must be demonstrated. You could join the community of other experts of coin collectors by following the guidelines.

The type of coin you collect will determine where you want to buy your coin. Some people organize their coins after discovering something unusual in their pocket change. Some people inherit coin collections, while some are introduced to coin collections by their friends or relatives.
Regardless of how you started your coin collection, you'll want to buy more coins to complete it, so you need proper education and planning for your collection.

Top Tips you Should Know Before Buying your Coins

Whether a beginner or a professional, you must consider a few things when buying coins. To avoid making a mistake while buying, it's essential to be informed. The few tips discussed in this section will help you understand how to get it right in your coin-buying process.

KNOW WHAT YOU ARE BUYING AND WHAT IT IS WORTH

Before buying any coin, you need to be familiar with the coin you want to buy. Look at how those coins are graded and identify if the coin has been cleaned or has any inconsistencies to know if it may be counterfeit.
You must understand your potential purchase and not get carried away by the flashy auction listing so that you won't spend more than your coin's worth. Instead, get familiar with the recent auction price, and make sure the coin is worth the price.

RESEARCH YOUR COLLECTION

Researching your collection before buying any coin is essential; you should know your coins' mintmarks, denominations, and grading systems. It will give you an edge in your buying process.

MAKE A PLAN

A plan and a budget will guide you on what to purchase. With your plan, you can see different sizes, presentations, and finishes available. Also, you can use the internet to research other companies that sell the coin you are interested in and study their prices, ranges, and offers.

Stick to your budget so you won't buy less. List the coins you need to complete a collection on a spreadsheet. Also, list the estimated cost of each coin and check if they align with your budget while buying; follow your list to avoid purchasing duplicated coins.

BUY COINS THAT INTEREST YOU

Many people ask, "What should I buy?" The answer is simple; buy what interests you. The fascinating design of the coin or the coin's history may interest you. Go through the internet, research the kinds of coins, choose the ones that interest you, and then ask companies about them.

Don't make the mistake of buying internet coins without researching because they may be counterfeit and overpriced. Instead, if you find a coin that you are interested in, learn about it. Your knowledge about the coin will help you avoid mistakes in your coin-collecting journey.

For example, the Lincoln Penny is rich and has great stories behind it. Also, some coins have a common theme, such as fish, buildings, queens, etc., which could interest you in a particular coin.

CAREFULLY HANDLE COINS AND STORE THEM PROPERLY

Although coins are made from metal, we believe metal is rigid. However, the coin's surface is delicate and can get damaged easily. In addition, the metals react differently based on exposure to the atmosphere around them.

Practice proper handling and storing your coins, as it will protect the value of the coins for many years.

Try wearing latex or cotton gloves if you want to handle your coin. If you don't have these items available, consider holding your coin by its edge. Don't try to clean your coin yourself; if you do, coin dealers will consider it damaged, and it will reduce the value of your coin and render it worthless.

JOIN A COIN CLUB

One best way to learn more about coin buying is by joining a coin club. There are many local coin clubs in different cities and towns. For example, the American Numismatic Association (ANA) is the country's largest organization dedicated to numismatic education. Regardless of your location, there are coin clubs that will meet your coin needs.

BUY FROM A REPUTABLE DEALER

Be sure to buy coins from a reputable dealer with a good track record by looking for dealers that have been in the coin business for several years and have a good reputation.

ASSESS YOUR COLLECTION

Once you've found a reputable dealer, you must assess your collection; a dealer can help you assess the coins.

WATCH ONLINE EXHIBITIONS

To properly understand your coin purchase process, you must check out coin-collecting exhibitions. Nowadays, these exhibitions are being conducted online, and you can learn from them. Moreover, you can connect with people with the exact coin you are interested in. You can ask your coin community members if you don't know how to get links to these coins-collecting exhibitions.

INVEST IN PROPER STORAGE

You may want to get storage for your coins. Ideally, you want them to be displayed where people can see them, but how you store them is up to you. Make sure you get a safe and secure place to store your coins.

The Best Places to Buy your Coins

Interestingly, there are different locations to begin your collection. Here are a few of them:

Coin Shops

To buy your coin, visit a coin store; a coin store is an important location to discover more about coin collecting. In addition, local coin shops are a great place to buy coin collections; they offer a wide selection of coins from different countries, and some of these coin shops specialize in coins from a specific region.

In addition, they have staff who are knowledgeable about the coins they have for sale, which can help you find the coins that fit your budget. At the local coin shop, you'll get valuable advice and assistance on the coin you are collecting. However, the coin stores could be expensive because they want to profit by selling their coins.

Online Auction Site

Online auction sites can be a great place to buy coin collections; many online auctions offer competitive prices and great deals on the coins. You can also read reviews about the auction site to ensure that you get a quality product. If you want to invest in uncommon coins, the best place to go is online auction sites.

Coin Shows

Coin shows are events where coin collectors, dealers, and other numismatists come together to buy, sell and trade other numismatic items. These shows are typically held in convention centers, hotels, or other large venues. It is an excellent place to buy your coins because you'll have more opportunities to meet other collectors and dealers, network, and learn more about the numismatic hobby.

eBay

E-Bay is a good place to find coins if the coin you want to buy is worth less than $1000. The rarest coins are found in major auction houses, but the expected dates are on eBay. If you are buying on eBay, you need some caution because there are mislabeled auctions, countless counterfeits, and coins with cleaning problems.

Social Media

The internet has made things easier for everyone. Thousands of coins are sold over social media platforms like Reddit, Facebook, and Instagram. Still, you have to be on guard to avoid falling into potential scammers and unreliable sellers' hands. If you have more understanding about your coin, then social media is a fit for you. In addition, it gives you a chance to form relationships with dealers across the country.

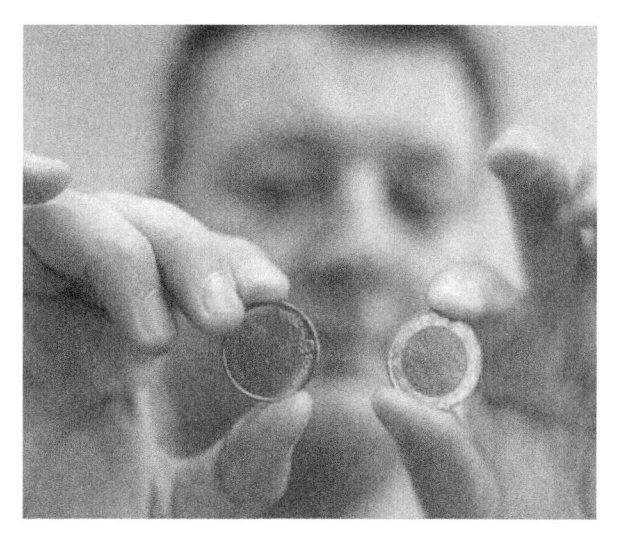

Flea Markets

You could try buying coins at a flea market because it's a fantastic spot to find unique coins. The only issue you might have with buying from this place is determining the coin's authenticity. But as a knowledgeable person in the coin-collecting industry, you might find it easy to identify unique coins. You only have to be careful.

Antique Shops

As a beginner, you can start with these stores. Some have online websites that showcase various catalogs that can help you decide which one to purchase. It would be best if you had someone guide you to know the authentic sites before buying anything.

Online Dealers

Another convenient place to buy coins for your collection is through online dealers. There are many online dealers on e-commerce platforms, and you can choose from them, but you need to confirm the authenticity of those online dealers. To buy the right coin, work with reputable dealers to avoid being scammed.

Common Mistakes to Avoid when Buying a Coin

Not Doing Your Research

One of the common mistakes that collectors make is not researching their coin collection. Before you buy a coin collection, you must research the coin and its values. Knowing the coin's grades and potential value will save you from overpaying for a collection.

Not Being Able to Identify a Fake Coin

Counterfeit coins are a significant issue in the coin collection industry; sadly, eagle-eyed collectors are occasionally duped today. To avoid being duped, inspect your coin and compare it to an example from a reliable source. Then, take a closer look at the coin; you can use a microscope to identify common counterfeit coins. Also, thoroughly research the coins in the collection to ensure they are authentic.

Buying from the Wrong Dealers

One of the costliest errors you can make is buying from the wrong dealer. To avoid this, ensure you buy from a reputable dealer who is educated on the nuances of numismatics. Also, remember to research the dealer before buying from them. Check for reviews and ratings to be confident that you are dealing with a reputable dealer. It is also essential to read the fine print on any sales agreement before making a purchase. This will help you understand any additional fees or conditions associated with the purchase.

Touching Coins with Your Bare Fingers

Treat your coins carefully and don't expose them to oil, dirt, and chemicals that may be on your hand. Instead, handle your coins with gloves or cotton cloth.

Not Having a Budget

Getting carried away when buying coins can be easy, so it's essential to set a budget before buying. When you have a budget, you'll avoid spending too much or buying coins you may not get dealers for.

Cleaning Your Coin

One mistake you shouldn't make, even if other collectors are doing it, is not to clean your coin. Coins are not clothes or cars; you should not clean them yourself. If your coins are discolored or damaged and need to be conserved, you can give them to numismatics professionals.

Cleaning your coin can reduce its collector value, and it's similar to restoring works of art which is the job of a professional who has the knowledge and experience of the techniques in cleaning the coin.

Questions to Answer Before Working with a Coin Dealer

While doing your research, there are some questions you should answer before doing business with any coin dealer. In this section, I have carefully explored a few of them. Getting honest answers to this question is instrumental to ensuring that you are working with the right person with the possibility of striking a good deal.

Is the Coin Dealer Experienced?

When it comes to coin collecting, it is vital to ensure that the coin dealer you are working with is experienced. The dealer is responsible for the accuracy of the coins you receive and can give you an accurate assessment of the coin's value.

Unfortunately, the fact is that not every coin dealer is experienced in the numismatics industry, so when you are buying your coins, you need a knowledgeable and reliable coin dealer. If you can't answer if the coin dealer is experienced, you might find it challenging to know which coin dealer to work with.

When you finally meet a coin dealer, introduce yourself and discuss what coin interests you. Then ask him some questions to know the type of dealer you are working with.

For example:
- How long have you been in this line of business?
- Are there any other fees involved? (It's important to ask if there are any additional fees associated with the purchase of the coin, such as shipping and handling fees. Knowing this can help you determine the final cost).
- Are you a member of the ANA or PNG?
- What methods of payment do you accept? (Knowing the payment methods accepted by the dealer can help you determine the best way to make your payment).
- Do you have an associate that we can work with?
- Do you offer appraisals or grading services? (It is essential to know if the dealer offers appraisals or grading services, as it can help you find out the value of your coins).

The answers you get will determine whether you should work with him. Note that if the coin dealer just began coin collection a few years ago, his knowledge may be minimal. On the other hand, if he is a member of PNG or ANA, it shows he has a level of commitment to ethical dealings with customers.

Does the Coin Dealer Have Adequate Assets?

When it comes to coin collecting, you must ensure the dealer you are buying from is reputable and has adequate assets to provide you with the coins you are interested in. In addition, you must know his financial stability in case of a dispute during your buying process.

Check to see if your dealer has insurance or a bond to protect against any losses that might occur. If a dealer cannot provide you with proof of insurance, then it's probably best to look elsewhere.

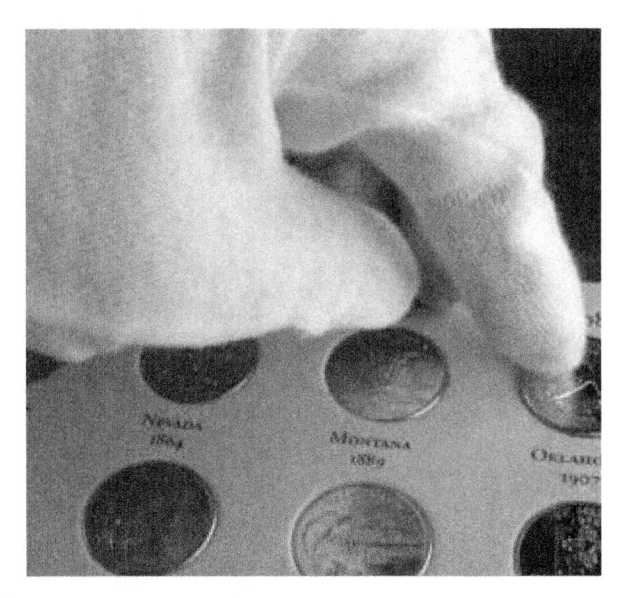

Is the Coin Dealer Known and Admired Among His Colleagues?

One of the best precautions you can take is to use a known, respected, or admired dealer among their colleagues. If a coin dealer has a bad reputation and is not respected among his peers, you shouldn't work with him.

A reputable coin dealer should have a good standing among his peers in the coin-collecting community and should be respected among other dealers. Although it might be challenging to identify a reputable coin dealer, you are safe if he is a member of a professional organization.

Also, you can talk to other coin collectors if they have had good experiences with the dealer and if they would recommend them. This will give you an idea of how respected the dealer is.

What Are the Coin Dealer's Ethics?

Coin dealers have the responsibility to uphold specific ethical standards when it comes to conducting their business. These ethical considerations are designed to ensure that coin dealers provide a fair and honest service to their customers while also protecting the interests of the coin community at large.

For example, one of coin dealers' most ethical considerations is providing accurate grading information. In addition, coin dealers should not take advantage of their customers by charging an excessive price for a coin.

Best Places to Find a Reputable Local Coin Dealer

If you are looking for a reputable local coin dealer, don't just type "coin dealers near me" because many people listed on the search engines under "coins" are jewelers, pawnbrokers, and others who do not study rare coins.

Even though it's easy to find a coin dealer, finding an honest and reputable coin dealer can be more difficult. So, to protect yourself, spend time researching before meeting a coin dealer.

Here are a few places you can find a reputable local coin dealer:

Coin Shows

If you cannot find a local coin dealer through the ANA or PNG, check if there are any local coins in your area. Attending local coin shows allows you to meet and talk with dealers and get to know them before making any purchases.

Coin Clubs

Coin clubs are a great place to connect with like-minded individuals who share an interest in coins. Through clubs, collectors can get advice on buying coins, learn about the history of a particular type of coin and get access to rare coins.

Many coin clubs also organize events and meetings where collectors show off their collections and trade coins with each other. At the coin club, you can get a reputable local dealer.

Professional Organizations

You can join a professional organization such as The American Numismatic Association because it's an excellent place for finding reputable local coin dealers. They have a directory of coin dealers vetted and approved by the ANA.

Referrals

Asking friends, family, and other coin collectors for referrals is an effective way to find a reputable local coin dealer. In addition, referrals can provide valuable insights into the quality of a dealer's coins and services.

Chapter 9
How to Make Money Collecting Coins

Coin collection is not solely for legacy or for the sake of having a hobby. You could use these valuables to make money as well. Coin collectors collect coins for different purposes.

Some of the reasons people collect coins include their aesthetic worth, historical value, scarcity, artistic value, and metal content. In addition, coin collectors gather coins by date, mint, country of origin, and condition. People also collect flawed coins because they appreciate over time.

In ancient times, it was common to give coins as presents on significant occasions. Coin collecting can be traced back to Greece, but some historians agree it started in Asia. The point is coin collection and exchange have been going on for a long time. Since then, collecting historic, rare items, including coins, has become an international leisure activity.

Coins have always been a source of income and will continue to be. Considering that many coins are manufactured from precious metals, particularly gold and silver, as well as the historical values and significance of coinage, it is the source of income for collectors and many individuals.

This chapter walks you through the process of making money with coin collecting.

How to Make Money Collecting Coins

Finish a Collection

Coins have a higher value when offered as a set. This is because completing coin sets was the original purpose of collecting coins before it became a profitable business. Therefore, several numismatists appreciate it.

For example, an ancient set of American coins in the Pogue collection set, dating from 1792 to 1840, was the most valuable collection sold and was sold for USD 200 million.

Self-Learning

Based on your enthusiasm for coin collection, if you intend to turn it into a lucrative business, you will need to research the industry and read a lot about it.

If you are well aware of a coin's physical features and historical symbolism, you are less likely to be scammed by con artists who sell counterfeit coins.

Purchase for a Discount

If you intend to earn money collecting coins, you must always employ your brilliant negotiating abilities when purchasing coins. You should not just buy something because the salesperson convinced you to.

Knowing the Grade of Coins

Knowing the grade and condition of the coins you buy helps you simplify getting the highest-grade coins gathered in a bag from dealers and coin experts.

Many coin collectors delegate their laborious and time-intensive chore of deciding the coin's grade to experts. These experts have honed their skills in determining coin grades. As a coin collector, it is pertinent that you are knowledgeable about the different coin grades.

Follow Auctions

Internet numismatic auctions help you trade rare coins without stepping outside your home. However, there are also live auctions in several locations. You can use a calendar to check for all the events hosted near your location.

Several coin collectors make the mistake of rushing into it too quickly because they are obsessed with finishing a coin collection and beginning another soon. To be an excellent coin collector, you must exercise patience and understand the industry. The most significant coin collections take time and experience to assemble.

There are occasions when you purchase excellent coins quickly, but such are rare. Never purchase a false coin when you require a coin to complete your set.

Adopt a Coin Collector's Mindset

Pure collectors only collect coins for their love of them rather than profit-making. However, they do their research thoroughly.

For instance, they keep themselves updated on the latest news concerning the coin they purchased. They don't purchase any overpriced coins during sales. No reason has been established for why experts don't purchase coins.

Establish Relationships

Getting information from dealers and collectors on issues like pricing, market dynamics, and trends is preferable. Building relationships with collectors help you get correct information. Most coin brokers and sales representatives only receive unreliable information when they go to events and occasions. Newsletters and coin periodicals can also be biased.

Learn Coin-Grading Techniques

Explore the Internet Marketplace

There are e-commerce platforms where a collection of coins will sell for a fair price.

However, since it is not a physical marketplace, you won't be able to feel it. Hence, your judging abilities depend on the description on the seller's page, customer reviews, and numismatic experience.

Make Connections and Join Groups

Joining online coin collection communities is a great way to expand your network and keep up with the latest information relating to coins. When you are with like-minded people, you become more comfortable asking questions and knowing more about your coin collection.

You can also exchange coins to complete a person's collection while completing yours. Some of those groups even offer free seminars on improving your coin collection skills and provide free resources and tools that might help you.

Create a Niche

Beginning a coin collection could be challenging if you do not have a niche or specialization. The best way to learn numismatics is to watch from a micro perspective, i.e., it is best to choose a particular perspective to be your focus. If you commit yourself to expertise, it won't take you more than a year to master it.

Do Not Lose patience

Some buyers make an error by buying rare coins for millions without understanding how to grade them. These types of collectors trust dealers and independent graders. Thus, causing a loss of money.

Do not buy particular coins if you are not confident about your grading abilities. Instead, examine all coins properly to determine their grade. You may attend auctions and exhibitions to observe them. If you trust any dealer or collector, you can also ask them for advice.

Think About the Future

Coins collection could be a horrible investment if you only want to make quick cash. Even if you purchase them at a retail price, you will pay more than 10% of the usual price. This means to break even you must wait for the price to increase by at least 10% before selling. To maximize profit, some coin collectors keep their coins for several years.

Prioritize Quality Over Quantity

Premium coins are costly because they are rare. Therefore, you should focus on selecting a few high-grade coins rather than many subpar coins. For instance, if your annual budget is $20,000, get four $5000 coins rather than twenty $1000 coins. Purchase the most excellent coins you can afford. Some of the greatest collectors recommend that your coins fit in a compact shipping box.

Buy the Most Expensive Coins You Can

As a beginner, you should buy less expensive coins until you have enough experience in the coin industry. Then, you can proceed to purchase expensive coins after gaining more experience and confidence.

Earn Money by Collecting Coins

If you have invested enough time and money gathering coins and experience, selling those coins after considering your investment is the best way to make money. I have discussed how to sell your coins in chapter eight. Please refer to it for a better understanding.

Money-Making Strategies Used by Top Coin Collectors

Coin collectors have employed many strategies to make money from their coin collection. Here are the top five strategies I strongly recommend for every beginner coin collector:

Buy and Hold

One of coin collectors' most traditional strategies is buying and holding the coins. For instance, in the stock industry, people buy coins and keep them until their value appreciates. They then sell them and make a lot of profit. However, this strategy is more suitable for long-term payers.

Buy Blue Chips

Blue Chips are coins whose value continually appreciates and have a broad target audience. They are usually popular among beginner-to-expert coin collectors. Due to their rarity, they never stop appreciating. Their value increases year after year.

This may be the coin for you if you are not looking for quick cash but a long-term investment.

Watch the Inflection Points

This strategy is similar to the stock market momentum recommended for collectors and buyers with some experience. Watching the inflection points involves buying the downgrade side of the rising inflation.

Inflection points are moments where demand increases and pushes the retail price up, sometimes even doubling it. If you are confident about your prediction of when it will happen, then you can wait for the perfect moment to sell your coins at a high-profit margin.

However, this strategy may not always work because it is believed that high-grade coins are fairly used.

Use a Large Collector Base

This strategy involves looking for, buying, and selling coins to the average collector. Employing this strategy will widen your target audience, help you buy and sell coins faster and make enough profits.

Using a large collector base only gets better with time and experience, so don't expect to make a high-profit margin.

Cherry-Pick

Rather than expanding your target audience, which was discussed in the previous strategy, using this strategy will narrow your target audience while trying to make the most out of the coin cycle movement.

This involves buying coins at their lowest and selling them to your buyers exactly when they are at their highest selling point. Profits can be made easily with this strategy.

Buy or Find

When deciding what to do with your coin collection, you can choose between buying and selling. Neither of the options affects the other. If you are buying coins, you are completing a set or investing for the future. If you sell your coins, you make money from your collection.

Each option could be satisfactory, demanding, or based on luck as you try to trade your coins.

Chapter 10: Top Mistakes you Should Avoid As A Beginner in Coin Collection

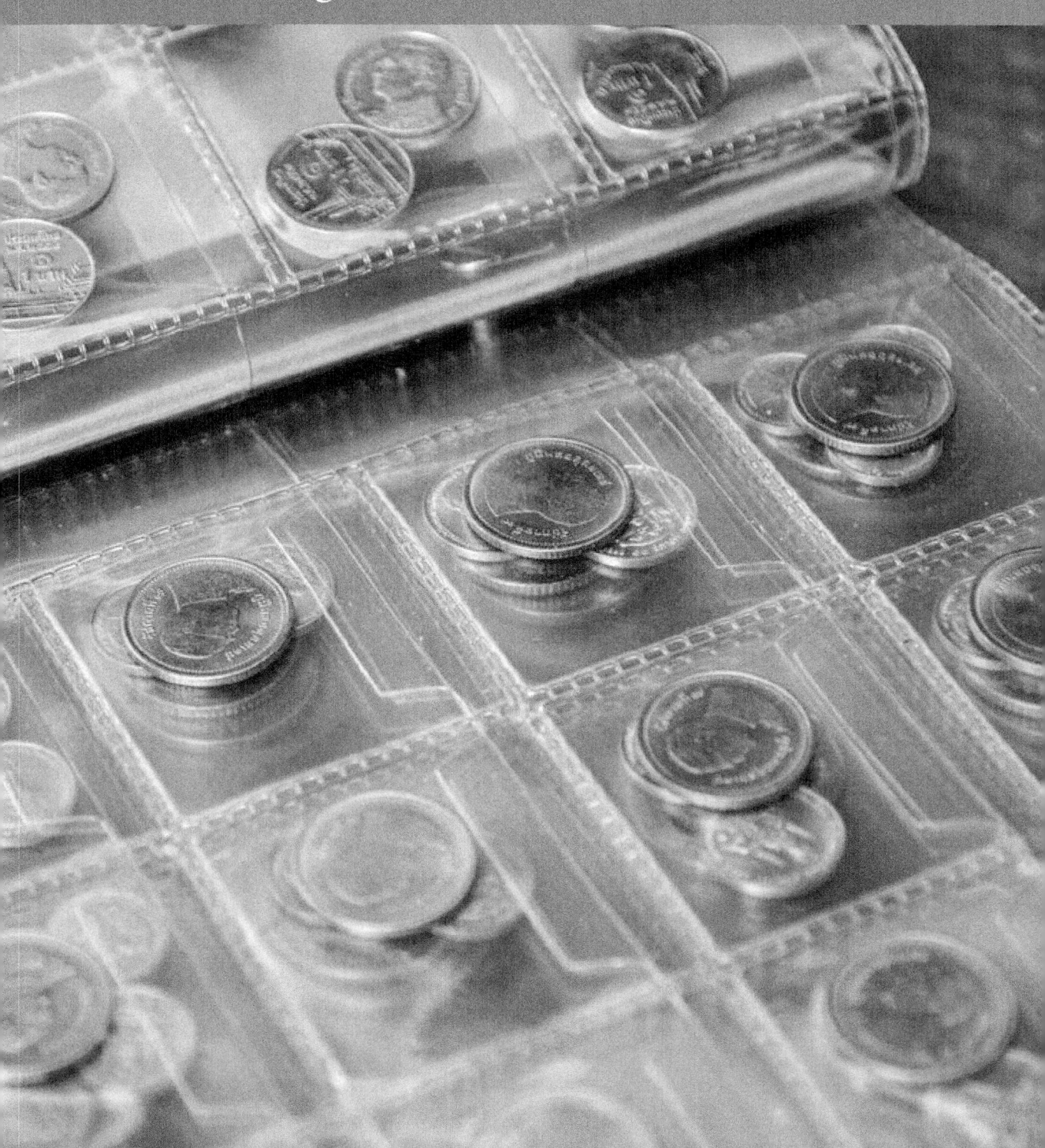

Many coin collectors lose money because of investment mistakes. As a beginner, you must take note of these errors, so you can avoid them.

TOO GOOD TO BE TRUE

Coins have detailed information that should be carefully checked to get the best deal possible when buying or selling your coin. However, it's typical not to pay attention to the details of your coins. This happens for several reasons, possibly because of its size, age, etc.

When buying coins, some collectors focus on getting a reasonable price. Aside from coin dealers and auctioneers, there are other places to get coins.

You might go into the market online, or physically, and find a "high-grade" coin selling at a low price. If it sounds too good to be true, then you need to be wary. Do not underestimate the importance of your experience in this regard, especially if it is a physical market. For an online market, consider using the seller's description and customer reviews to confirm the truth.

FOLLOWING THE LATEST TIPS

Many people predict the next excellent coin every other day. As a beginner, make no mistake by investing based on predictions. If predictions were easy, many of these people would be wealthy. Therefore, you should only invest when you are very confident about it.

IMPULSIVE COIN COLLECTING AND BUYING

Understanding the specifics of a new hobby requires time, and coin collection is not exempted. For instance, when you want a rare coin, you should be able to grade its authenticity and how much it should cost.

Knowing little about a coin will only lead you to buy low-grade and costly coins impulsively.

NOT BEING ABLE TO IDENTIFY COUNTERFEIT COINS

No manufacturing industry is immune to counterfeit products. Unfortunately, the numismatic community is also not excluded from this, as you can find counterfeits everywhere, even in the big stores. This is why you should take your grading seriously as a beginner because it is easy to be duped when you know little about the industry.

BUYING COINS FROM TV DEALERS

When people do infomercials, it may be unreal and solely based on profit. The advertisers may even repeatedly claim that they provide the best value for coins. Experts say this is a tactic to encourage ignorant collectors because the cost of advertisements is more than that of the product.

There is no guarantee that those coins are appropriately graded, even if the dealers claim they are. Even when these TV dealers claim that they are offering NGC- or PCGS-graded coins, you can't ascertain the state of the coin when it left the NGC or PCGS compared to when you see the infomercial.

As a beginner, don't fall for their tricks. Instead, collect coins only from trusted dealers or members of your group.

MAKING FUTILE INVESTMENTS

Low mintage or very low mintage is a trendy attribute of valuable coins because of the many interests in rare metals. Mintage is the total quantity of a coin that the mint produced. However, having a specific coin with a low mintage doesn't mean it is rare.

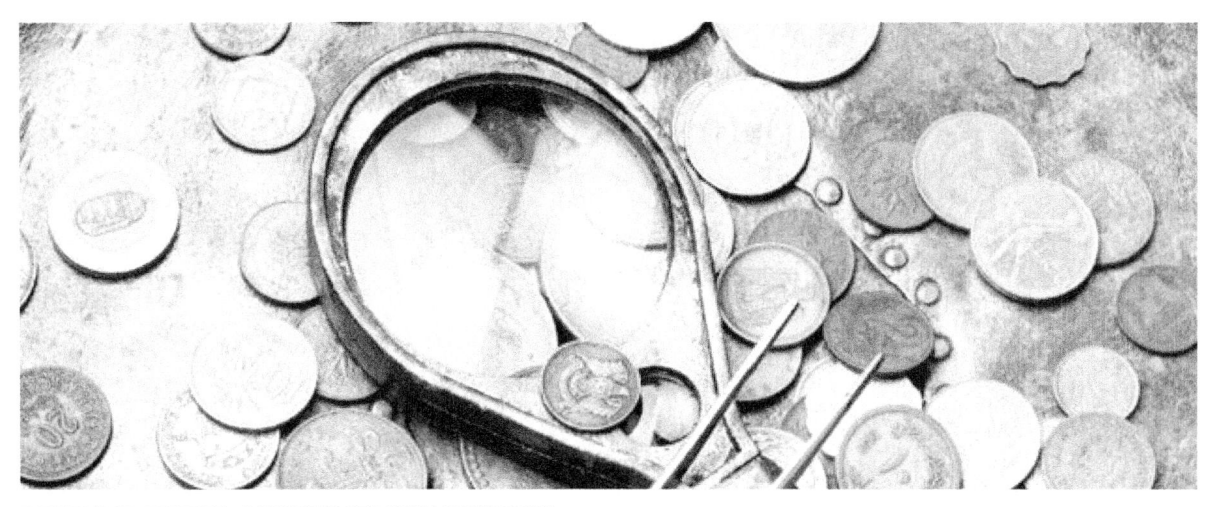

BUYING CERTIFIED COINS FROM SELF-SLABBERS

Coins found in slabs do not automatically mean rarity or perfect condition. The NGC and PCGS are the two top authentication and certification companies.

SKIPPING THE RESEARCH

Many beginners believe that coin trading is just buying and selling coins of historical significance. However, if you want to be successful in the coin industry, you cannot afford to skip the research aspects of it.

It would be best if you also remember that understanding the industry will take a lot of time and patience, so don't rush the process. Otherwise, you risk running into losses occasionally.

Knowing standard information about coins, such as the average buying price and what coins to buy, won't get you far. As you grow your collection, you must also expand your knowledge and experience in studying coins.

CARELESSNESS

There have been incidents of people cleaning old coins and destroying them. Coins aren't like antique cars that should be buffed to shine and look clean. Aggressive and abrasive chemicals will tarnish your coins, so it's best to give them to professionals to clean if necessary.

It is also believed that your hands can gradually damage coins because of the natural oils in human skin. Therefore, to prevent skin oils from damaging coins, it is best to wear gloves before touching them, as discussed in chapter nine.

FOREIGN COINS FROM UNKNOWN COUNTRIES

Every country has its sovereign right to produce its currency. Some lesser countries will issue limited edition coins with famous coinage. Although low-mintage coins may be shown as rare, this does not imply value and market.

Many other factors determine the value of a coin. Therefore, looking out for them before collecting the coins is advisable. Also, avoid coins covered in precious metals such as gold and silver.

Chapter 11
Myths and Facts About Coin Collection

Thanks to the historical value of coin collection, both as a hobby and as an income stream, there have been several misconceptions that have grown over the years. Understanding these myths and knowing their associated facts is instrumental to ensuring you are starting coin collecting on the right foot.

This chapter carefully examines the common and not-so-common myths that you should know to help you become a better version of yourself as a beginner coin collector.

Interesting Myths About Numismatics

Here are a few of these interesting myths about numismatics:

COLLECTING RARE COINS IS ONLY FOR RICH PEOPLE

Coin collection is often regarded as the "hobby of kings." This notion has gone on for centuries, and the ancient Romans are known for collecting Greek coinage. For almost 2000 years, European kings and royalty have been known to have collected coins. Many of the most excellent museums have founded their collections on these coins.

However, today, coin collection has been turned into a democratic affair. Coin collection, especially for high-grade coins, can be challenging but fun. You can start your collection from pocket change in malls before looking for rare coins within your budget. There are exciting coins for every budget. It is possible to have just one rare coin in your collection.

Remember that coin collection is a significant investment, and the long-term accumulation of rare coins is a worthy investment.

OLD COINS ARE THE MOST VALUABLE

Several factors determine the value of a coin, and age has almost nothing to do with it. Ancient Roman coins can be bought between $5 and $10 if they are not rare. Some time ago, a gem 1956 Franklin Half Dollar, sold at an auction for over $100,000. The prominent factors determining a coin's value are rarity and condition.

When you have these two combined in a coin with other factors, your coin is set to sell at an outrageous price. The popularity of the coin is also an essential factor. An 1895 Dollar is said to be worth $75,000, yet several hundred are known. Also, when coins have great stories attached to them, they become more valuable.

CLEANING COINS MAKE THEM MORE VALUABLE

Cleaning your coins with an aggressive chemical will damage them. Coins must be given to professionals for cleaning, but most rare collectors disagree with this. Instead, they insist on buying uncleaned coins with excellent eye appeal. In truth, these coins are a result of expert conservation.

MINT ERRORS ARE USUALLY RARE AND VALUABLE

The 1943 Bronze Cent, like other rare coins, is expensive. However, most coins are standard and not very valuable.

RARE COINS ALWAYS GO UP IN VALUE

As good as this sounds, it is not valid. Most long-term investors collect coins, but investing can be very tricky. The rare coin market is a cycle and leaving the collection over the long term sounds safe. Instead, find a trusted person with experience to help you with your coin collection. A trusted advisor can help you use the down market to your advantage.

LIMITED EDITIONS OF MINTED COINS ARE RARE

Many people have bought limited coins from private mints or limited-edition US government-minted coins in velvet boxes. They are sold in perfect condition, or as the first release, and are considered pristine, thanks to their color, beauty, and history.

These heavily marketed coins have excellent eye appeal. They have high grades from reliable sources, new and unused. Sadly, they are not rare, and you may not find out until you get an evaluation, and it may be too late by then.

You may be wondering why they aren't rare. Old coins minted in currency and used in the trade may not be found in perfect condition. This is because they were not designed to appeal to commercial buyers. These coins are not limited by design but by loss or deterioration. Therefore, it is rare to find them in good condition.

Indeed, rare coins are valuable, but it is hard to find them in perfect condition.

SEMI-NUMISMATICS ARE RARE COINS

Many coin dealers and resources claim that semi-numismatics are just like rare coins. This is not true. Semi-numismatics could be a great addition to your metal portfolio because some coin dealers sell them and give them out as a bonus. The Morgan and Peace Silver Dollars are good examples of popular semi-numismatic coins.

Although they add value above the actual price and may act as a dual investment, they are not rare. Their value will rise and fall alongside other precious metals, not with the taste of collectors. Semi-numismatics have their place but if you want precious coins, go for rare coins.

While semi-numismatics can be an alternative to an ounce of silver or gold, they should be regarded as metals, not rare tangible assets.

IT IS ALWAYS GOOD TO BUY COINS FROM CATALOGS

Firstly, this is not true, not even in the least. There are examples of so many people whose worst coin-collecting experience was from catalogs. An unpopular saying goes, "If you can add it to your shopping cart, then it is not rare."

Some collectors make the mistake of spending a large amount of money on catalog coins with beautiful packaging. Taking this huge risk is not advisable. A glossy catalog with an elegant gift box may get you into trouble.

THE BEST DEALS ARE FOUND ONLINE

This is similar to myth nine. The truth is good deals can be found online but not always. There are fakes and overpriced coins as well. Always remember that if it is too good to be true, then something is not correct. It is critical to know who you are buying from online.

RARE COINS ARE TIED TO BULLION PRICES

Supply and demand play a more significant role in the value of rare coins than gold and silver bullion prices. The bullion price of gold truly has an impact, but rare coins have gone up in value even when gold prices were flat.

COIN COLLECTING IS A GREAT WAY TO MEET GIRLS

This is hilarious, and I hate to break it to you, but it is an absolute lie. Coin collecting may not be a way to meet the girl of your dreams, but it is undoubtedly a way of making new friends. When you join coin-collecting groups and meet people with like minds, it makes it easier to make friends, and what better people to make friends with than those who share your interests?

Numismatic friends are also an essential aspect of being a great collector. Many of these people have been collecting for years and would love to share ideas and tips.

Interesting Facts About Coins

- Coin collecting can be traced back thousands of years. Because of its roots, it is often regarded as "the hobby of kings." This is not because of the cost of collecting coins but because this hobby started with kings.
- Coin tossing to determine two possible outcomes started in the time of Emperor Julius Caesar. Romans called this "the game of chance:" Navia au caput (ship or head), which referred to the prow of a ship on one side and the emperor's head on the other.
- In ancient Rome, the emperor's word was the law and final say. So if you played this game and the coin landed heads up, you had to do the emperor's wish. In Britain, this was called cross and pile. It took its name from the indentation of the device used to press the metal as the coin was struck.
- The first international coin collectors' convention was held in August 1962 in Detroit, Michigan. Over 40,000 collectors attended. American Numismatics Association and The Royal Canadian Numismatic Association sponsored the convention.
- In 2002, Euro coins first came into use; however, 135 billion Euro coins were in circulation. Globally, there are 1 trillion coins in circulation.

- The world's most extensive circulating library of numismatic material was founded in 1891 and is called the American Numismatic Association.
- Not only wealthy people collect coins. Some coin dealers will allow the purchase of coins at a little less than face value. You can purchase some coins for as low as $10.
- You may buy a coin from United States Mints. In addition, there are catalogs filled with commemorative coins, sets, and other items of interest for coin collectors.
- Florence, a city in Italy, was the first to mint its gold coins. It was in 1252. The Fiorin became known as Florence, then as Florin.
- The first Roman coin ever found in Britain was a silver coin aged 2,224 years old. The coin dates back to 211 BC. One part of the coin depicts the goddess of Roma and the mythical twins, Castor and Pollux, and their horses on the other side.
- The oldest coin was found in Ephesus, a city on the coast of Asia Minor. The coin is more than 2,700 years old and is one of the earliest. The ancient coin was hand struck.
- There are public displays of numismatics collections all over the world.
- Saint Eligius is the patron saint of numismatics, born around 588, and he lived in France. He was a metal worker and died around 659.
- The first coin minted in Britain dates back to the Iron Age. They were made in silver, gold, and bronze between 1 BC and 1 AD.

Conclusion

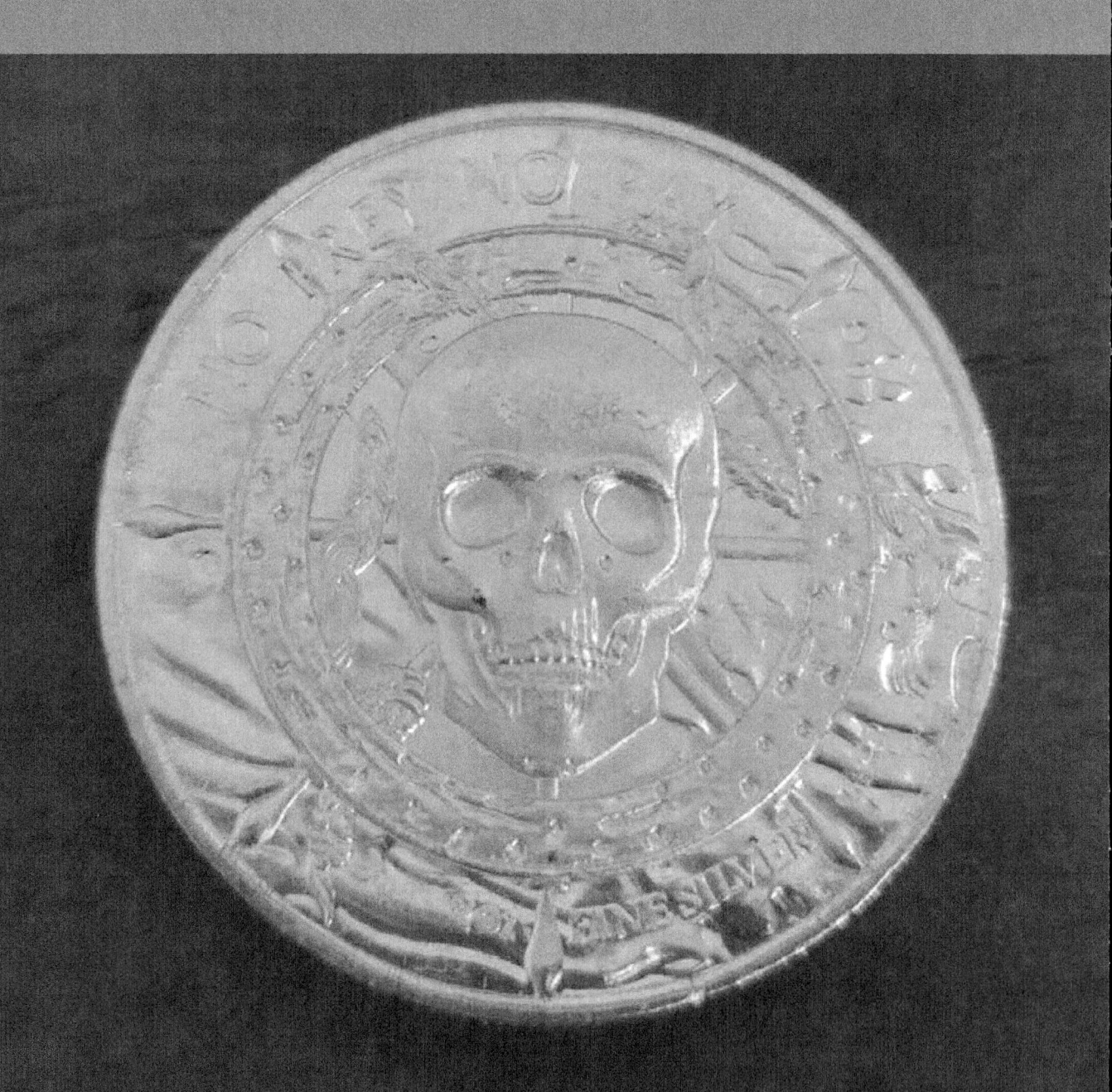

Trust me, coin collecting isn't rocket science. However, it can be more if you do not understand the intricacies associated with the hobby-turn-money-making scheme.

Thankfully, in this guide, I have carefully examined everything you must know to not only get started on the right foot as a beginner but also find the hobby as exciting as possible while looking to make money from it in the long run.

Coin collecting can be fun and profitable, but it can also get you burned if you follow certain trends. And that is why chapter eight, where I discussed the common mistakes you should avoid as a beginner coin collector, is important.

Where to sell and when to sell your collected coins shouldn't be a worry any longer, as I have also discussed that in this guide.

I sincerely hope you found this book helpful in achieving your coin collecting dreams.

Cheers!

GERALD J. ROBINSON

Printed in Great Britain
by Amazon